Penguin Modern European Poets
Advisory Editor: A. Alvarez

Yannis Ritsos: Selected Poems

Yannis Ritsos was born in Monembasia in 1909. His first
collection of verse, *Trakter* (*Tractors*, 1934) brought him to the
forefront of the new poetic movement in Greece of the
1930s. He has published about forty volumes of verse of
which the best known are: *Epitaphios* (1936; parts of which
have been set to music by M. Theodorakis); *To Tragoudi Tis
Adelfis Mou* (*My Sister's Song*, 1937); *Earini Sýmfonia*
(*Summer Symphony*, 1938); *Dokimasia* (*Trial*, 1943); *Ydria*
(*Pitcher*, 1957); *To Dentro Tis Fylakis Kai I Gynaikes* (*The
Prison Tree and the Women*, 1963). Ritsos's poetry is intensely
lyrical and is often coloured by his left-wing sympathies. He
blends modern poetic techniques and conceptions with
traditional diction and forms successfully. He was arrested
during the military *coup* of April 1967 and deported to an
island prison. Since 1967 he has continued his extraordinarily
prolific output, and has completed at least six new collections
of poems which were only recently allowed to be published
under the present régime in Greece. Selections of his poetry
have appeared in translation throughout the world, particularly in
all East European countries and in Germany, Spain, Italy, France,
Switzerland, Sweden and the United States.

Yannis Ritsos has received a great number of international
distinctions, the most recent of which were the International
Prize for Poetry, awarded in Belgium in 1972, and his
election as member of the Academy of Sciences and
Literature of West Germany.

Ritsos, Giannēs

Yannis Ritsos:
Selected Poems

Translated by Nikos Stangos
with an Introduction by Peter Bien

To our Marco,
the "grecian"
friends
Cleo + Giorgos

Athens
Greece
1975 (June).

 Penguin Books

Penguin Books Ltd, Harmondsworth,
Middlesex, England
Penguin Books Inc., 7110 Ambassador Road,
Baltimore, Maryland 21207, U.S.A.
Penguin Books Australia Ltd, Ringwood,
Victoria, Australia
Penguin Books Canada Ltd,
41 Steelcase Road West, Markham, Ontario, Canada
Penguin Books (N.Z.) Ltd, 182–190 Wairau Road,
Auckland 10, New Zealand

First published 1974

Made and printed in Great Britain by
Richard Clay (The Chaucer Press) Ltd,
Bungay, Suffolk
Set in Monotype Bembo

Contents

5

from *Testimonies C* (1966–7)

Acknowledgements

A few of these poems, in these translations, first appeared in the following magazines: *The Times Literary Supplement*, *Modern Poetry in Translation* and the *London Magazine*.

The following poems were first published in Yannis Ritsos, *Gestures and Other Poems 1968–1970*, Cape Goliard, London, 1971: 'Unfinished', 'After the Defeat', 'And Narrating Them ...', 'The New Dance', 'The Decline of the Argo', 'Penelope's Despair', 'In the Dark', 'At Least the Wind', 'Indisposition', 'Before Sleep', 'Enumeration', 'Dissolution', 'The Third One', 'Inside and Outside the Window', 'Reversal', 'Awaiting His Execution', 'White Landscape', 'Departures, III', 'Circle', 'A Three Storey House with Basement', 'In the Void', 'The Essentials', 'Conscious', 'Desertion'. Permission to reprint any of the above poems should be addressed to Jonathan Cape Ltd.

I should like to thank A. Alvarez, Peter Bien, David Plante, Alex Tzonis, Annie Lee and Jennifer Skidmore for their invaluable comments on my translations; they are responsible for such improvements that the end-product is as much theirs as mine. Finally, I would like to express all my gratitude to Yannis Ritsos, without whose patience, help and love this book might have never come to be.

NIKOS STANGOS

Introduction

Speakers of English have appreciated the Irish literary revival almost since its inception, but have been much slower to recognize an equally extraordinary florescence in Greece. One reason, obviously, is that Modern Greek is not only a foreign language but a 'minor' one; nevertheless, more people keep learning Greek, and more translations keep appearing. Cavafy, Seferis and Kazantzakis are now widely known; Myrivilis, Palamas, Sikelianos, Elytis, not to mention younger figures such as Vassilikos, have also received some attention. How extraordinary, then, that Yannis Ritsos, who for decades has been acknowledged inside Greece as one of the undeniably major figures of her literary revival, and who has been increasingly recognized on the Continent, should be so new to the English-speaking world. And how nice to meet a fresh voice which is also a fully mature one, a 'new' poet with an entire career behind him!

A few of Ritsos's poems have of course appeared recently in English and American periodicals, and a small collection, *Gestures and Other Poems 1968–1970*, was published by Cape Goliard in 1971. But the present volume is the first attempt to offer, in English translation, a general and representative selection of Ritsos's work which aspires to give a sense of this poet in his totality. When we realize the extent of Ritsos's writing (the three-volume *Poiímata 1930–1960* runs to 1,500 pages and is itself only a selection) we can appreciate the translator's difficulty in choosing what to include. Anyone familiar with Ritsos will know at once that the present volume does not span the poet's full career chronologically. Indeed, the earliest work offered here dates from 1957, whereas Ritsos's writings go back to 1930. This means, as well, that several of the most famous poems, works which established Ritsos's reputation in Greece, are omitted. What Mr Stangos has attempted to do, however, is to span the poet's entire career in a more subtle way: aesthetically and thematically instead of chronologically. The poems offered here as representative have been chosen to show the diversity of Ritsos's forms – in particular, the interesting combination of short poems and extremely long ones; the variety and range of his modes – elegiac, lyric, and narrative; the fluctuation, yet deeper constancy, of his attitudes. Hopefully, the multiplicity contained in this selection will suggest its own unity and therefore be an accurate, though miniature, portrait of the artist, one which reveals an integrated poetic personality.

The poems in this volume are generally simple enough on their surface to be 'available' to the average reader even on first perusal. Thus, certain individual characteristics of Ritsos's art may be perceived without difficulty, and we may then add these together in an attempt to comprehend the poet's totality. For example, even on a first reading we are immediately aware of how well Ritsos evokes the everyday life of contemporary Greece. We see before us an album of snapshots, not so much of things especially photogenic as of people, places, and events that are completely ordinary and prosaic: a quick plunge into the sea on a deserted beach; a sick man listening to music from a nearby taverna; a driver guarding the load of water-melons in his stalled lorry and combing his hair as some girls admire him on the sly; old fishermen sitting behind the brine-stained windows of a sea-side café; rotting fruit; gleaming whitewash under sunlight; a woman cleaning string beans while a corpse lies in the back room; a seamstress closing her shutters at nightfall, her mouth full of pins.[1] No sooner, however, do we establish Ritsos's tireless alertness to the minutiae of life in the Greece of today than we realize his equal interest in the Greek past. Throughout his work, but especially in the collection *Repetitions* (the generic title is significant), there are poems with historical or mythical subjects – the Peloponnesian War, Theseus, Ariadne, Penelope – poems which seem quite different in tone and intent from the simple

1. See the following poems: 'Noon', 'The Day of a Sick Man', 'Working-Class Beauty', 'An Old Fisherman', 'Death at Carlovassi', 'A Three Storey House with Basement'.

evocations of contemporary life, and which constitute a second approach to reality. If we look still further, we find that the contemporary and the historical, though separated in certain poems, are fused and indeed deliberately *con*fused in certain others, with the result that we have still a third aesthetic approach, one perhaps most characteristic of Ritsos, where apparent simplicity and apparent lucidity coexist with mystification, complexity, even nightmare. *The Dead House* exemplifies this most strikingly, for in this Pirandellesque mélange of eras, the narrator is both an aged Electra reciting the horrendous events of her father's return to Mycenae, and an aged recluse of modern times recalling the piano and silverware of her once-elegant home, as well as the return of soldiers from some twentieth-century war, their under-shirts full of lice. In the shorter poems too, a radio next to the Argives' tent at Troy, or an incongruous statue in an otherwise contemporary landscape,[2] remind us of Ritsos's ability to comprehend hellenism in its entirety, and to use diverse elements in order to create effects which make us uneasy, despite our continuing conviction that the poetry, though more complex than we first imagined, is still simple enough to be comprehended by the average reader.

All these characteristics should also remind us of the essential role played by metaphor in Ritsos's work. Shelley, in a celebrated passage in his *A Defence of Poetry*, claims that poetic language by its very nature is 'vitally metaphorical', and then goes on to define the metaphorical element in a way which bears on Ritsos: 'It marks the before unapprehended relations of things and perpetuates their apprehension, until words, which represent them, become, through time, signs for portions or classes of thought instead of pictures of integral thoughts . . .' This definition helps us to see the various ways in which metaphor operates in Ritsos's verse, ways which correspond to the three approaches described earlier, and which, similarly, move in the direction of complexity and mystification. In so far as Ritsos merely evokes the minutiae of everyday life, we have a splendid metaphoric capacity that

2. See 'Necrography' and 'Recollection'.

aids this evocation by shocking us into strong sensual awareness. Normally, the tiredness of language and of our own powers of observation prevents us from hearing, seeing, or touching as well as we might. But when a metaphor or simile convincingly relates 'before unapprehended' elements of seeming incongruity – when, for example, a shriek remains

> . . . nailed in the dark corridor
> like a big fishbone in the throat of an unknown guest

– we hear that shriek, see that corridor, and feel the sound's entrapment as never before. This is vitally metaphorical language at its most obvious. If we move to Ritsos's historico-mythical mode and remember the key word 'repetitions', we will realize that a poem such as 'After the Defeat', ostensibly about the Peloponnesian War, is really a metaphorical treatment of other defeats more recent, with a relation established between one element that is mentioned and another that is not. The aesthetic effect of this kind of metaphor begins to be complicated, because here we are being led to an awareness of those portions or classes of events which lie beneath the individual event described. By means of metaphor, the poem offers a universal statement about history, or at least about Greek history. Lastly, in so far as Ritsos fuses and confuses the past and present, the metaphorical element becomes more subtle still. Poems employing this third approach make us uneasy because we feel that we ought to understand them, yet know that our understanding must go beyond (or beneath) either simple sensual acuity or simple historical insight: that the external world, whether present or past, is supplemented by something else. Hopefully, then, our uneasiness will enable us to see that the metaphorical linkages in such poems are between outer and inner, physical and psychic, that the external materials serve as entrées into the poet's internal fears, hopes, wounds, dreams – the configuration of his soul. And it is here, of course, that we realize to what an extent the simplicity of Ritsos's work is deceptive.

In adding together these individual characteristics with the hope of comprehending the poet's totality – of feeling an integrated poetic personality – it may be most helpful to think of Ritsos as a painter rather than a writer. If nothing else, the printed words on the page speak much more to our eyes than to our ears. (I say 'the printed words on the page' because the poems, when *recited* properly, do indeed speak to our ears; but this auditory effect comes primarily from rhythms and euphonies, not from subject matter or imagery.) Even when sounds are evoked, the similes employed tend to be visual, as for example that shriek nailed in its corridor like a fishbone in someone's throat. More importantly, many of the poems are graphic scenes from hellenic life – I called them 'snapshots' earlier, but they are much more like paintings than photographs, because Ritsos's language adds texture, and because he is able to arrange line and colour to suit his own aesthetic needs, his aim never being simply to reproduce external reality as such. Even when these scenes are complex and have a narrative plot, so that one might wish to speak of Ritsos as a story-teller or dramatist rather than a painter, the poems are still essentially graphic and relate more to the pictorial than the theatrical arts, because the complexity – the unfolding detail of the narrative – is captured in a single moment and fixed, as on an ancient frieze or urn. In certain at the more subtly pictorial works, the point may not lie in the narration at all. 'Of the Sea', for example, introduces us to a man cutting up a fish on the wharf. There is much blood involved, and two women remark how well the reddish gore suits the man's handsome black eyes. Then the focus shifts to a street above, where children are weighing out fish and coal on the same pair of scales. If this poem were a snapshot, we would justify the children on realistic grounds, and remark Ritsos's accuracy in observing the details of Greek life. If the poem were a story-teller's narrative, we would look for some rational (or even irrational) progression from the wharf to the street, some causal links between the man, women, and children. But perhaps the poem is primarily a painting. As such, it asks us not to proceed in time from the wharf to the scales, but to see both simultaneously, as when we view the two levels of an

El Greco, or of a Byzantine icon. Furthermore, it asks us to note, as the primary 'meaning' of the poem, nothing more than a visual metaphor marking the before unapprehended relation between the red and black below, emphasized to such a degree by the women, and the red and black above – bloody fish and sooty coal being weighed on the same pair of scales. In short, the poem challenges us to see better. Ritsos, having responded to life with a painter's eye, gives us a small equivalent for life and asks us to respond in the same way.

The more one explores Ritsos's work in terms of this analogy with painting, the more one senses how the poet operates, what drives him, where his uniqueness lies. He is considered rare, for example, because he cultivates both long and short forms, and because he often works simultaneously on both. But the short poems are either distillations from the longer ones or preparatory sketches: an archive of experiments, ideas and observations which will be put to subsequent use in a 'grand canvas'. (One thinks as well of the epiphanies of that other eye-oriented artist, James Joyce – sudden spiritual manifestations, 'whether in the vulgarity of speech or of gesture or in a memorable phase of the mind itself', obsessionally recorded and then systematically inserted in the larger works.) Perhaps the nature of sketches is that they should be suppressed, and indeed critics tend to accuse Ritsos of publishing too much, especially when they compare him to a writer at the other extreme, Cavafy, whose sanctioned works fit within one thin volume. Yet Cavafy, for all his greatness, lacked Ritsos's compulsion to observe and register every nuance of external reality; his imagination was dramatic and historical rather than pictorial, and therefore his sketches, unlike Ritsos's, could not be preserved simply as witnesses, however slight or tentative, to the voraciousness of an eye preying continually on life's colours and forms. The analogy with painting helps us to understand Ritsos's extraordinary prolificness (a poem a day, sometimes several in a day) as well as his decision to publish so extensively, because although not every one of these poems can be a masterpiece, there is no more reason to discard them than there would be to destroy, say, a tiny, hurried sketch of an ugly harridan by Rembrandt, or a sculptor's repeated attempts, with paper and charcoal, to get the shape of a hand just right before attempting it in marble. If we apply the analogy with painting we begin to realize that Ritsos's value lies not so much in those particularly successful poems, large or small, which will become or have already become anthology pieces, as in the totality of his work including the slighter poems, for this totality is what demonstrates most unmistakably his extraordinary aesthetic drive: the artist's urge to observe life, record it, transform everything into beauty.

It would be wrong, however, to apply the pictorial analogy too narrowly lest it darken and distort rather than illuminate. The emphasis on graphic re-presentation, with the eye focused on *external* reality, gives us an incomplete Ritsos, one much more limited than the poet displayed in this volume. I have already stressed that Ritsos's simplicity is deceptive, and that perhaps his most characteristic poems are precisely those in which apparent lucidity coexists with mystification. If he is a realist he is equally a surrealist; indeed, one of his favourite practices is to give us a perfectly observed scene which suddenly, at the end, turns insane: for example a seaside 'barbershop' where fishermen walk in one door to be shaved, and then walk out the other with 'long reverent beards'. Or we have the deliberate confusion of historical eras already mentioned, or poems in which the realistic element is more or less effaced in favour of dream-vision or nightmare ('Way of Salvation' and 'Association' are examples). Yet even in the most mystifying of the poems, the visual quality perseveres; there is always a scene, a graphic concreteness, and this leads us to extend the pictorial analogy rather than to abandon it. What we must realize is that Ritsos's aesthetic drive – the need to observe perpetually and to create on the basis of that observation – has directed his vision inward as well as outward. In this he is of course hardly singular; one might say that the dominant trend in both poetry and prose during Ritsos's formative period between the two World Wars was this inwardness.

Far from being eccentric, he exhibits characteristics which place him within the dominant 'ism' of that time: expressionism, which has been defined as 'a probing search for a deep emotional reality behind appearances – a reality that the artist finds by observing his own subjective reactions, and for which he then fashions an adequate and equivalent formal means to evoke a similar response in the viewer'.[3] Ritsos is not just an expressionist – like many writers or painters with long careers he has progressed through various styles, and like any artist of true worth, must be defined ultimately only in terms of himself – yet to consider him part of this school helps to remind us of the degree to which he works from subjective reality, looks inward, establishes metaphors which mark the relations between matter and psyche and which become signs not only for the inner landscape of one particularly sensitive man, but for all men who share Ritsos's love of life and who have been injured, as he has, by forces which deny life. In short, as he wrote in 1946 in a poem called 'The Meaning of Simplicity',

> I am behind simple things, hiding, so that you may find me;
> if you do not find me, you will find the things,
> will touch what I touched with my hand;
> the tracks of our hands will converge.
>
> . . .
>
> Each word is an outlet
> for a meeting (often postponed).
> The word is real when it insists upon the meeting.[4]

This simple statement about simplicity helps us to find the complexity lurking behind Ritsos's work. His poems either direct us inward to a psyche obscured by the outward things described, or direct us outward to an external reality validated by the poet's touch. They actualize the ideal and at the same time idealize the actual. Their energy is vitally metaphorical in that

3. Peter Selz, *Emil Nolde* (New York: Museum of Modern Art, 1963), p. 38.

4. *Poiímata 1930–1960*, Vol. II, p. 453.

they are always arranging meetings between opposites, whether those opposites be self and other, psyche and matter, poet and reader, or subject and object. Yet all this multiplicity and complexity is unified within an integral personality, because the poet Ritsos, whether turning outward or inward, whether impersonal in approach or intensely personal, whether definite in his moral positions or radically indefinite in front of life's intricacy, is always a bridge. His career has been a relentless insistence upon meeting.

Since the method of this volume is to provide a representative selection of Ritsos's poems on aesthetic and thematic rather than chronological grounds, and since the poems here offered cluster in the last third of Ritsos's career, it is appropriate that we attempt, however telegraphically, to survey the poet's background and development. Not surprisingly, this survey will lead both inward to Ritsos's personal life and outward to the political life of his country and era.

Whichever way we look, the story is not a happy one. The great calamity of Greek life, the defeat in Asia Minor, occurred in 1922 when Ritsos was thirteen years old. His father, a well-to-do landowner in Monemvasia, was ruined by this event, and Ritsos spent his adolescence in the decaying family mansion (cf. *The Dead House*) in an atmosphere of sickness and death. His mother and brother had both died of tuberculosis a year before the Asia Minor catastrophe; after it, his father went insane, as did one of his sisters, somewhat later. Ritsos, having finished his secondary schooling, moved in 1925 to an Athens swollen with destitute refugees from Anatolia, all looking for work. After short spells as a typist in a law firm, a clerk for a notary public, and a calligrapher producing law diplomas, he too contracted tuberculosis and was forced to spend three years in the Sotiria Sanatorium in Athens, followed by an additional cure in Crete. Returning to the capital and unable to secure any other employment, he finally placed himself – ashamedly – as a dancer in a theatrical troupe. But these setbacks did not debilitate Ritsos's spirit. At a time (1928) when another Greek poet, Karyotakis, committed suicide out of despair with himself and the world, Ritsos was finding ways to sustain himself. These were two: poetry and socialist revolution. His first slim volume, *Tractor*, in which he collected poems from the period 1930–34, begins with a call to Mother Poetry to receive him, and ends with effusions against a rotten, decadent society which will doubtless abuse and insult him and his verses: the mirror in which the common people will finally discern their true features. Between this prologue and epilogue are excruciating and almost embarrassingly personal poems about his own humiliation by the 'hordes of barbarians' who surround him; about his father, incarcerated in an asylum while his son addresses him wearily from the Sotiria Sanatorium; about the acolyte of Art, Beauty and Ideas who is forced to rattle a tambourine for a few drachmas. There are also hymns to Marx, Engels, and Russia, as well as calls for one world in which all men will be brothers.[5] The same dual orientation – personal and political – continues into Ritsos's next volume, *Pyramids*, published in 1935. An impassioned elegy dedicated to his sister uses the occasion of her deteriorating mental condition to speak of the illness which ravaged the entire family; another elegy directed at his own unhappy boyhood ('O, I do not remember ever being young; / Like a paralysed old man I would hide indoors reading ancient books . . .') concludes with a vision of himself as a common soldier among the ranks of the workers, fighting on their behalf with 'lyre and knowledge'.[6]

These early collections are the journeywork of a precocious and gifted youth who still had not found his distinctive voice. The dedications – to Karyotakis, Sikelianos, Palamas – show that Ritsos was reading in contemporary Greek literature and looking for models; the poetic forms – sonnets, impeccable hendecasyllabic or hexametric quatrains rhymed *abab* – show that the prototypes he chose were still the traditional ones of Italian and Greek prosody. On the other hand, these early volumes are a true

5. See *Poiímata 1930–1960*, Vol. I, pp. 9, 59, 16, 21–2, 13, 31, 58.
6. See ibid., pp. 82–7, 102–5.

part of Ritsos's canon, not just juvenilia, because they do establish his abiding attitudes and also give occasional premonitions of later techniques such as impersonal narration. Conversely, though he was later to don a mask of impersonality to cover the naked 'I' of much of the early verse, his mature poetry has remained intensely personal and autobiographical, as can be seen in the present selection, and though the unquestioning faith in particular political saviours was to be modified later by obeisance to the word 'perhaps', the remainder of his career has continued to display energetic devotion to the ultimate goals of freedom, justice and brotherhood for all men. The unified diversity of personal/political established in the two first volumes endures in the subsequent career, as does Ritsos's vision of the role which the poet must play in society. We may also look upon these early volumes as prophesying his own destiny, for Ritsos has indeed fulfilled the responsibility he announced forty years ago when he offered himself to Mother Poetry; and society, in turn, has fulfilled its 'responsibility' by abusing him, insulting him – and worse.

These early years, though still scarred by the débâcle of 1922 and its social and economic consequences, were excitingly fruitful ones in Greek intellectual circles. The nationalistic afflatus which had sustained Palamas and his generation was no longer possible; the 'Great Idea' of occupying Constantinople and re-establishing Greece as the dominant force in the eastern Mediterranean was so completely dead that everyone realized the need for new directions, new ideologies. Some turned to international communism, others to the chastened humanism of countries which had experienced an equal débâcle in 1914–18. Both turnings had consequences for poetry in Greece, helping it to renew itself. Those with allegiance to the proletariat insisted on extending the domain of 'the poetic' to objects and environments meaningful to the working class (note the title, *Tractor*, of Ritsos's first volume); those with bourgeois orientations turned their attention, in a similar way, towards eliminating inflation, rhetoric and irresponsible lyricism from Greek verse, since all of these were now out of keeping with post-1922 Greek reality. In addition, they looked abroad, to France in particular, and imported into Greece the autonomy, subjectivism and fragmentation which was western Europe's poetic response to the breakdown of older certainties. The 'generation of the thirties' in Greece, stimulated by these foreign trends (and also by the pioneering sarcasm of Karyotakis and the weary irony of Cavafy), effected an important change in Greek poetry. The great year was 1935, which saw the publication of Seferis's *Mythistorema*, the début of Elytis, and the inauguration of Greek surrealism by Embeirikos.

It is against this background that we must view Ritsos as he struggled to find his distinctive poetic voice. He found it in 1936 with *Epitaphios*, a long poem which has remained his most celebrated work and is now in its tenth edition. A year later he reinforced this new voice so strongly with *The Song of My Sister* that Palamas himself addressed a quatrain to Ritsos in which he hailed this bitter elegy – in it the poet laments his sister's definitive insanity – and concluded: 'We step aside, Poet, that you may pass.'[7] By 1937, therefore, Ritsos's career had been launched with the ultimate imprimatur. *Epitaphios* and *The Song of My Sister* taken together – the one drawing from political events, the other from private – are representative of much that followed. Both, for example, are elegiac in tone and content, yet at the same time offer hope: the one affirms Revolution, the other Poetry. In both, Ritsos began to discover a way to continue the lyricism of predecessors such as Palamas, but to make this lyricism a responsible confrontation with the problems of post-1922 Greece instead of an escape into self-pity, and also to wed his lyrical impulses to the precision exemplified by anti-lyricists such as Seferis and Cavafy. In *The Song of My Sister*, furthermore, Ritsos liberated himself from rhyme and from metrical strictness, embarking on the free verse which has remained his normal vehicle. However, in neither poem did he liberate himself entirely from rhetorical élan or from what Peter Levi has aptly called 'the temptation to draw his passion larger than life-size'.[8]

7. *Poiímata 1930–1960*, Vol. I, p. 185.
8. *The Times Literary Supplement*, 10 March 1972, p. 273.

These purgations were to come later, especially when Ritsos discovered the dramatic monologue style exemplified in *The Dead House* and when, in the shorter pieces, he began deliberately to squash his flights beneath a mask of impassivity, a neuter expression occasioned by disdain, or tolerance, or perhaps both.

Before looking ahead, however, we must dwell a little longer on *Epitaphios*. I spoke earlier of Ritsos's musicality: the rhythms and euphonies which make his work auditory, when recited, as well as visual. This poem is lyrical in the basic sense of that term: 'meant to be sung'. Robert Frost once declared that a true poem memorizes itself; by analogy we might say that a true lyric sings itself, hankers after a melody – and *Epitaphios* does precisely this, its words seemingly vaulting off the printed page in order to dance upon a musical staff. What is crucial to note is that Ritsos achieved this lyricism by grafting his earlier elegiac mode, and also his political fervour, on to the root stock not now of a foreign model but of Greek folk-song, the *demotikó traghoúdi*. Employing a fifteen-syllable line and rhymed couplets, he preserved the feel of this superb form: its verve engendered by weariness and hardship, its uncanny back-reaching into the racial and mythical past of a people continually invaded, cheated, and raped. Lyricism became viable because Ritsos's afflatus, controlled by the pattern and spirit of folk-song, no longer projected merely his own experiences, nor buttressed the poem with fantasies of success either private, racial or atavistic, but instead held it rooted in the palpable earth of national tragedy, yet without losing hope.

Epitaphios is overtly political, and as such has had a 'political career' of its own. If nothing else, it shows us the inconstant seas – now murderous, now buoying – which Ritsos himself has had to travel. In May 1936, workers in the tobacco industry in Salonika (a city whose proletarian quarter had been one of the focal points of communism in Greece for at least a decade) went out on strike to protest unfair wage controls. Police were called in; they fired on the unarmed strikers, killing twelve and wounding hundreds. The next day the newspapers carried a photograph of a mother, clothed in black, weeping over her dead son as he lay on a Salonika street. Moved by this photograph, Ritsos set to work immediately. The dirge which he produced after two days of intensive creativity, wedding his emotion to technical skill, places this particular tragedy in a larger perspective to give it meaning and provide a mirror in which the common people might discern their true features. Though equating the tragedy with Christ's crucifixion (the Epitaphios is the sepulchral lament sung in Greek Orthodox churches on Good Friday) the poem moves at the end from crucifixion to resurrection, thus enclosing sorrow in the sweetness of the poet's abiding hope that injustice may be overcome. At first the bereft mother grieves inconsolably for her son:

> Μέρα Μαγιοῦ μοῦ μίσεψες, μέρα Μαγιοῦ σὲ χάνω

> A day in May you left me, a day in May I lost you

She cannot understand why he died, cannot understand his political convictions; but gradually she changes, and at the end, encouraged by her vision of a future in which men shall be united in love, she vows to carry on his struggle:

> Γιέ μου, στ' ἀδέρφια σου τραβῶ καὶ σμίγω τὴν ὀργή μου,
> σοῦ πῆρα τὸ ντουφέκι σου· κοιμήσου, ἐσύ, πουλί μου.

> My son, I'm off to join your comrades and add my wrath to theirs;
> I've taken up your gun; sleep now, sleep, my son.

The event which this poem celebrates was part of the unrest that led to the Metaxas dictatorship several months later, and when that régime made clear its intellectual orientation by publicly burning books in front of the Temple of Zeus, Ritsos's volume was of course included. Though not re-published during the two ensuing decades, which saw not only Metaxas's government but also the German occupation of Greece and then two civil wars, this naturally musical poem eventually achieved the widest possible audience when Mikis Theodorakis set the dirge to music in the late fifties, employing the quintessential instrument of the people, the bouzouki, and using rhythms which 'carried on the tradition of the elegiac threnody found in the klephtic ballads, the songs of Epiros, the dirges of Mani, the songs and dances of the islands, and the Cretan *rizitika*'.[9] This setting, precisely because the bouzouki was at that time condemned in fashionable circles as the instrument of brothels and hashish dens, called forth intense debate, with the result that the music penetrated all segments of Greek society. Ritsos's yearning for poetry which would be known not only to intellectuals, but to dockhands, fishermen and taxi-drivers, was fulfilled. In addition, the poem became a kind of unofficial 'national anthem' of the Greek Left. For example, when in 1963 another tragedy occurred – also in Salonika, also in May – and hundreds of students kept vigil outside the hospital where the parliamentary deputy Lambrakis lay dying after being murderously assaulted by political thugs, it seemed inevitable that the mourners should sing Ritsos's *Epitaphios* in their martyr's honour. The dirge was also chanted through the streets of Athens after the deputy's funeral at the same time that the slogan 'Lambrakis lives' began to appear on every wall. Most recently, this same poem has been presented in dramatic readings in England as a protest against the Colonels. *Epitaphios* lives.

From 1936 until 1952 Ritsos was unable to publish freely, for political reasons. Making the best of his restrictions, he cultivated his lyrical gift at first with intensely personal subjects, as in *The Song of My Sister*, but then increasingly shifted his attention from himself to others, and also to nature itself. As an early, partial, step in this direction, *The March of the Ocean* (1939–40) continues Ritsos's earlier theme of Poetry as a bulwark against misfortune, but recognizes that the strength to resist comes not so much from the poet's individual will in isolation as from that will drawing power from the constancy of sun and sea, the 'inexhaustible song of nocturnal waves', a song which refuses to

9. George Giannaris, *Mikis Theodorakis: Music and Social Change* (New York: Praeger, 1972), p. 132.

yield to night or to sleep, and which enables the poet, in his turn, to cry: 'What if they leave, if everyone leaves. Let them. / I shall remain / across from wide heavens / across from grand seas / without bitterness or complaint – / to sing.' [10] This early emphasis on heroic collaboration between man and nature was to bear fruit several years later in *Romiosini*, Ritsos's tribute to the Greek Resistance, where the landscape itself is seen as the principal resister, and where the shift from self to other becomes complete.

Meanwhile, Ritsos not only cultivated his lyricism in long poems such as *The March of the Ocean*, but continued to experiment technically, especially in the short or medium-length poems which, characteristically, he was writing at the same time. Two collections of these, covering the years 1935 to 1943, move all the way from Whitmanesque verse-paragraphs ('A Summer's Midday Dream') to a two-line haiku ('April'). Though the lyrical and elegiac modes remain strong, some of these poems lean towards the colloquial diction, staccato rhythms, general simplicity, and elliptical bareness that dominate Ritsos's post-war style.

As the political situation turned from bad to worse, Ritsos increasingly favoured overtly political subjects which rendered immediate publication unthinkable. In the winter of 1941–2 Greece was in the clutches of the severe famine which followed Hitler's invasion of the country the previous spring. Mussolini had been repulsed by the Greeks' remarkable campaign in Albania, and the spirit which made that campaign possible, though now temporarily exhausted, was already preparing to resist by means of guerrilla warfare and underground subversion, in order to bring about the country's resurrection. Ritsos did not take to the mountains, his tuberculosis having denied him the necessary robustness, but, identifying himself clearly with EAM – at first a coalition of various resistance groups, later dominated by the far left – he began to fight with his pen, producing a long series of poems which circulated clandestinely among the resisters and buoyed their spirits. An example is 'The Final Century B.H.';

10. *Poiímata 1930–1960*, Vol. I, pp. 289, 276.

here, Ritsos looks forward to a new era comparable to that begun by Christ, and sees himself – the poet – as a link between old and new, a forerunner who points the way. Written in the summer of 1942, when nature, at least, had revived herself after the bleakness of the previous winter, the poem celebrates the heroes of the Albanian Campaign, weeps over the invasion and famine, rejoices that E A M has been formed, and ends with a sign placed at the crossroads: 'This way to the sun', and also the hope that in the future, when people pass freely beneath the sunlight, someone will wonder who painted that sign 'with such awkward letters' and someone else will recall that it was 'Yannis Ritsos, poet of the final century *Before Humanity*'.[11] Another poem which looks at a future resurrection, despite the darkness of 1942, is 'The Burial of Orgaz'. Here, Ritsos builds his metaphor upon El Greco's two-tiered painting where surmounting a sombre burial are the effulgent heavens, with an angel already delivering Count Orgaz's inchoate soul to Christ. Packed in on the lower level of Ritsos's own canvas are mutilated veterans of Albania, innocent Athenians dying from the famine, resisters executed by the Germans; on the upper level (the springtime which will come 'tomorrow') are workers building a new road. They are naked to the waist, barrel-chested, modern replacements for El Greco's strikingly naked John the Baptist who kneels at Christ's feet. But whereas the miracle of El Greco's painting is the integration of earth and heaven, death and life-everlasting (heaven itself descending resplendently in the persons of Saints Stephen and Augustine to lay Orgaz in the tomb), in Ritsos's poem – in Ritsos's Athens of 1942 – the Below and the Above are sundered. Applying metaphor over metaphor like a graphic artist working with layer upon layer of paint, Ritsos speaks of the 'ladder' which ought to unite winter with spring. But the ladder does not exist. Why? Because our mouths, which ought to be sounding the trumpets of salvation, are 'stuffed with silence'.[12] The implication, if we unite the two metaphors, is once more that the Poet, especially in

11. ibid., Vol. I, p. 521.
12. ibid., Vol. II, pp. 203–4.

times when men's hands are tied, may be a ladder or bridge to a better world, and that the material with which he constructs his bridge is Song. We might add, paraphrasing Peter Levi, that perhaps life too, like El Greco's painting, has its dual levels, and that while prisoners and active resisters under an oppressive régime save a people's honour, poets such as Ritsos save a people's soul, because they keep delivering a nation's idealism, however unformed or inchoate its state, to the judgement of Humanity. In any case, this poem, like 'The Final Century B. H.', uses Christian allusions to assert Ritsos's ultimate faith not in Christ or anything supernatural but in man's best instincts, at the very time when man's worst instincts were temporarily ascendant. The poem is also of interest technically, because it combines complexity of reference – personal experiences, contemporary events, historical or legendary memories, previous expressions in art – with simplicity of language.

Everyone in Greece hoped that resurrection would come as soon as the Germans withdrew. Instead, the sundering of native inhabitants from foreign rulers was replaced by a worse sundering of Greek from Greek. In the first Civil War, which followed almost immediately after Liberation, the leftist-dominated Resistance was routed, in December 1944, with the aid of British tanks. This defeat of EAM's hopes was then exacerbated by repressive measures applied against all radical and liberal elements in the turbulent years which followed, years which only increased the schism between right and left, and devolved into the second Civil War. During the interim period (1945–7), Ritsos joined with other artists in appealing to the United States, Great Britain, and the Soviet Union to recognize what was happening in Greece; more importantly, he set to work on his magnificent tribute to the defeated resistance-fighters and, beyond them, to all previous and future strugglers for Greece's freedom. Appropriately called *Romiosini* ('Greekness'), this tribute sees the men who fought against the Germans and afterwards in the first Civil War as national heroes easily equated with the free besieged of Missolonghi during the War of Independence; with that legendary stalwart of medieval times, Digenis Akritas; or with the epic giants celebrated in folk-song:

and when they danced in village squares,
ceilings shook in the houses and glassware rattled on the shelves

. . .

They treated Death to a raki served in their grandfathers' skulls;
on those same threshing-floors they met Digenis and sat down to dinner
slicing their sorrow in two as they used to slice their barley-loaf on their
  knees

. . .

On the threshing-floor where one night the stalwarts dined,
the olive stones remain and the crusted blood of the moon
and the fifteen-syllable verse of their guns.[13]

Though eschewing the actual decapentasyllables of *Epitaphios*, that earlier celebrative elegy in folk-song metre, Ritsos in this later poem continues the spirit of the *demotikó traghoúdi* with its back-reaching into the racial past of a people – the Romioi – who, despite wave after wave of invasion by foreign troops or usurpation by un-romaic Hellenes, have remained the only true proprietors of the Greek landscape – itself celebrated as the prime resister – and whose ever-renewed energy is the strongest bridge to an improved future. So the poem, though occasioned by disillusion and chastened in tone, is also both defiant and hopeful. It ends by invoking a tomorrow in which others will recognize that the Resistance wished to bring love to Greece, not hate, and its final word is 'brothers'. Though this tomorrow is not yet visible, the poet articulates the certainty of trees, stars and men that it shall appear, and asks his brothers, in effect, to keep vigil: to wait for it, watch for it, just as one watches over a corpse in the certainty that the soul will be delivered to 'God's heart'.

Romiosini could not be published when it was written. It

13. *Poiímata 1930–1960*, Vol. II, pp. 65, 62, 68.

appeared some years after the second Civil War, in 1954, and was reissued in 1966, whereupon Mikis Theodorakis composed settings for several sections, once again bringing Ritsos's verse to an extremely large audience – just before the works of both Ritsos and Theodorakis were banned by the régime of 21 April 1967.

By the time of the second Civil War, Ritsos had grown sufficiently dangerous to the Right to cause his imprisonment. Arrested in 1948, he was sent for detention to Lemnos and then to the infamous 'Institute for National Re-education' on Makronisos, where the guards administered physical and psychological torture in an attempt to transform communists into 'good Hellenes'. Lastly, he was transferred to Agios Efstratios. Though released at last because of ill-health, he was picked up again in 1951 and detained for an additional year. The four years in these various concentration camps did not, however, silence him. On Makronisos he placed his poems in a bottle which he buried in the stony ground; on Agios Efstratios ('Ai Stratis') he was able to recite his works to his fellow prisoners – which explains the straightforward style employed during this period. Probably the most celebrated individual piece is the 'Letter to Joliot-Curie', dated November 1950, a poem which was smuggled out of Greece at the time, unknown to its author. It begins:

> Dear Joliot, I am writing you from Ai Stratis.
> About three thousand of us are here,
> simple folk, hard workers, men of letters,
> with a ragged blanket across our backs,
> an onion, five olives and a dry crust of light in our sacks,
> folk as simple as trees in sunlight,
> with only one crime to our accounts:
> only this – that we, like you, love
> peace and freedom.[14]

As always, Ritsos's prime witness during these years of national and personal suffering was his continued faith in Song as

14. *Poiímata 1930–1960*, Vol. II, p. 99.

a bridge to decency, a faith reinforced by what he observed in nature, though not always in human nature. 'Ah yes,' he sighed in another poem composed on Agios Efstratios,

> Ah, yes, the world is beautiful. A man beneath the trees
> wept from the joy of his love. He was
> stronger than death, that man – which is why we sing.
>
> . . .
>
> No one will silence our song. We sing on.
> The world is beautiful, we insist
> – beautiful, beautiful, beautiful – and we sing on.[15]

One might say that these words of affirmation were written with clenched teeth, with the tinge of cynicism and bitterness that begins to darken Ritsos's later poems, although it never wholly dominates the hopefulness at their core. But faith in the poet's role remains, as does faith in a better future, and that is why an entire series of poems from the dark period 1941–53, including *Romiosini* and 'Letter to Joliot-Curie', was brought together in 1954 under the generic title *Vigil*, beneath an epigraph by the poet of another dark period in Greece's history, Dionysios Solomos: 'Forever open, forever vigilant the eyes of my soul.' Again, the implication is that we keep watch over a corpse, confronting all of life's degradation and injustice not with despair but with hope. Ritsos had been doing this, of course, ever since his very first poems in *Tractor* and *Pyramids*, but he had also grown in the meantime because of the outward circumstances which had fused his own personal misfortunes with those of his people, and because of his inner capacity to extend his elegiac and lyrical gifts to communal subjects.

When Ritsos was released in 1952 he returned to Athens to begin a crucial period of happiness in his personal life and development in his artistry. The return was celebrated exultingly in a long bitter-sweet poem entitled *Unsubjugated City* and in a short lyric called 'Peace', written in January 1953. Dedicated to

15. ibid., p. 133.

Kostas Varnalis, this latter work defines its subject by invoking life's simplest and most genuine pleasures:

Peace is the odour of food in the evening,
when the halting of a car in the street is not fear,
when a knock on the door means a friend

...

Peace is a glass of warm milk and a book in front of the child who
awakens[16]

The poem is included at the end of the collection *Vigil* as though to vindicate Ritsos's – and Greece's – faithful waiting throughout the preceding years; it also looks forward to Ritsos's own happiness, for in 1954 he married and in 1955 welcomed an infant daughter into his household and sang her arrival in a 'small encyclopaedia of diminutives' called *Morning Star*, the first poem addressed to a member of his immediate family that was not a dirge. These happy events, however, were not enough to erase from Ritsos's life the huge sense of loss which had predominated hitherto; nor had the political situation in Greece, however improved, suddenly become idyllic for a man of Ritsos's persuasions. What we see, therefore, in this next crucial period of artistic development is a continuation, basically, of Ritsos's previous concern with the everyday world of Greece, with his own and his nation's past, with memory and dream, and with social and moral revolution, but also an attempt to make his approach to these subjects more reflective, tentative, responsive to the blatant contradictions and complexities in his experience. We see him moving towards dramatic monologue as a favourite method, because this form lends itself both to reflection and to objectivity; we see him leaning more heavily upon myth alone or myth fused, or deliberately confused, with contemporary events, as a way of universalizing and depersonalizing his themes; we see him preferring the pronouns 'he' or 'you' to the pronoun 'I'. All these tendencies are well illustrated in the present

16. *Poiímata 1930–1960*, Vol. II, p. 173.

selection, and we need not describe them any further here, except to reiterate what was stated earlier: that the style perhaps most characteristic of Ritsos in his later work is one which makes apparent simplicity and lucidity coexist with mystification, complexity, nightmare. We should also add that Ritsos, a poet not normally given to theorizing in prose about his verse, has nevertheless issued in recent years some crucial statements of intent. In an unpublished introduction to *Testimonies* broadcast in Prague in October 1962, he spoke about his growing consciousness of all that is 'vague, perplexing, incomprehensible and directionless in life . . .', about his desire to hide the tragic element of the poems behind a 'mask of impassivity', about his love for the words 'perhaps' and 'or', his fear of rhetoric, his continuing gratitude for everything that life has to offer, and his unshaken belief that the role of ar t is to transform negation into affirmation. In another introduction, this time to a volume of his translations of Mayakovsky (1964), he reaffirmed the positions just cited and placed them against a backdrop of chastened experience. 'We have learned how difficult it is not to abuse the power entrusted to us in the name of the supreme ideal, liberty,' he stated, 'how difficult not to lapse into self-approbation in the name of the struggle against individualism . . . The first cries of enthusiasm and admiration have given way to a more silent self-communing.' These two factors, taken together, have led modern poets to a self-examination which is at the same time self-effacing and hesitant. Thus their reliance on the third person; on dramatic narrative rather than exclamation; on reflection directed towards the past or towards an enlarged field of vision which refuses to speak of the future without considering past and present as well; on language which aspires to the tone of a simple, confidential conversation out of fear of being understood, or of not being understood . . .[17] Perhaps one of Ritsos's poems says all this even

17. These excerpts from the Mayakovsky introduction are available in French translation in the Poètes d'Aujourd'hui series, no. 178: *Yannis Ritsos*, Étude, choix de textes et bibliographie par Chrysa Papandréou (Paris: Éditions Seghers, 1968).

more forcefully. Called 'The Disjunctive Conjunction "Or"',
it comments on a passage from the *Iliad*: '. . . Then brazen Ares /
bellowed as loud as nine or ten thousand / warriors in battle . . .'
'O that "or",' cries the poet, that

equivocal smile of an incommunicable and uncooperative wisdom
which turns mockingly towards itself and others,
knowing full well that precision
is impossible, does not exist (which is why
the pompous style of certainty is so unforgivable – God preserve us
   from it).[18]

The period from 1953 to Ritsos's re-arrest in 1967 was an
extremely productive one in which he published no less than
twenty-eight separate collections of new work, not to mention
three large volumes of his *Poems 1930–1960* and nine volumes of
translations. In 1956 he received official recognition – a tardy
complement to the unofficial recognition awarded him earlier
by the public and by critics such as Palamas and Kleon Paraschos –
when his *Moonlight Sonata* won the National Prize for poetry.
The Prize also gained him recognition outside Greece; after the
poem was translated into French, Louis Aragon eulogized Ritsos
in the following terms:

. . . C'est un des plus grands et des plus singuliers parmi les poètes
d'aujourd'hui. Pour ma part, il y avait longtemps que quelque chose ne
m'avait donné comme ce chant ce choc violent du génie . . . D'où vient
cette poésie? d'où ce sens du frisson? où les choses telles qu'elles sont
jouent le rôle des spectres . . . Il y a, dans cette poésie, le bruit . . . d'une
Grèce qui n'est plus cette de Byron ou de Delacroix, d'une Grèce qui est
sœur de la Sicile de Pirandello et de Chirico, où la beauté n'est point des
marbres mutilés, mais d'une humanité déchirée . . . la décadence d'une
époque.[19]

18. In the collection *Repetitions*, dated 18 June 1969. *Pétres, Epanalípseis,
Kinglídoma* (Athens: Kedros, 1972), p. 91.
19. *Les Lettres Françaises*, 28 February–6 March 1957, p. 1.

As a result, Ritsos suddenly found himself an international celebrity, at least in the socialist world. In 1956 he journeyed to the Soviet Union, after that to Hungary, Bulgaria, Czechoslovakia, Romania and Germany; in 1966 to Cuba. Meanwhile, inside Greece, he continued his 'testimonies' in active as well as poetic ways. One example will suffice. When the Bertrand Russell peace movement spread to Greece, Ritsos became one of its advocates along with Theodorakis and the parliamentary deputy Lambrakis. In April 1963, the Greek Committee for Peace organized an Easter march from Marathon in imitation of Lord Russell's Aldermaston marches. Ritsos participated in this, and was among the two thousand who were consequently detained by the authorities. We have already spoken of Lambrakis's fate a month later in Salonika, but it should be noted as well that Ritsos, together with Theodorakis, personally joined the vigil held for the dying deputy outside the university hospital, when *Epitaphios* was sung.

Given this continuing activism on top of the earlier allegiance to EAM, not to mention the fact that some of Ritsos's works had been adopted by progressives as central articulations of their ideals, it is hardly surprising that the poet was among those arrested on the very first night of the 1967 coup or that his writings were promptly banned. Once more he found himself in various detention camps, this time for a period of a year and a half, followed by exile in Samos, where contact with the outside world was denied him and he was prevented from accepting invitations extended by the Festival of Two Worlds at Spoleto, for example, or the Arts Council of Great Britain. Eventually, owing certainly to protests from abroad, the government did release him, and even granted him a passport, but with restrictions which Ritsos felt he could not accept. Besides, he knows that in the years left to him – his health has remained precarious – he must stay in Greece, close to the language and the people that have formed him. So he lives now in a depressing neighbourhood of Athens in a street called Koraka ('Crow'), observing the life around him:

> Dental surgeries have multiplied in our poor suburb,
> so have chemists, coffin makers ...
>   ... A tap
> has been forgotten running all night at Crow's sidestreet
> in front of the flowershop, the barbershop.[20]

He concentrates on 'The Essentials':

> Did you eat your bread? Did you sleep well?
> Were you able to talk, to stretch your arm?
> Did you remember to look out of the window?

'Athens 1970' is not the same as the unsubjugated city which Ritsos greeted so exultingly upon his return in 1952. Then, to be sure, there was hunger – old ladies scrambling in the marketplace for soup-bones, blinded veterans playing accordions on street-corners – but there was also the hope and impetus born of hunger: 'Mothers, the bread-troughs are waiting for you to knead loaves of peace.'[21] People had a voice then, an audible voice, whereas now, when they are no longer hungry, their hunger has been replaced by aimlessness, by the futile bustle of humans without ideals:

> ... they are in a hurry
> to go away, to get away (where from?),
> to get (where?) – I don't know – not faces –
> vacuum cleaners, boots, boxes –
> they hurry.

As for the poet himself:

> You must tighten your tie. Like this.
> Keep quiet. Wait. Like this. Like this.
> Slowly, slowly, in the narrow opening, there
> behind the stairs, pushed against the wall.[22]

This is where a long life of personal and communal vicissitude has left 'Yannis Ritsos – poet of the final century B.H.' He is free

20. From 'Desertion'.
21. *Poiímata 1930–1960*, Vol. II, p. 266.
22. From 'The Meaning Is One'.

now in body as he has always been in spirit, having survived imprisonment, exile, misunderstanding, isolation and disillusion – as well as adulation, perhaps the greatest trial of all. Measured against such hardships, the bitterness of his recent poems is scarcely excessive, especially when we feel, as we continually do, an optimistic and affirmative energy still at work. And, of course, we have much to be thankful for. True, there is still no ladder uniting winter with spring (will there ever be? does such a ladder exist?); true, the mouths are still stuffed with silence. But precisely because of repeated disillusion, precisely because the wheel of crucifixion-resurrection-crucifixion has kept turning so inexorably in Ritsos's life, and in Greece's, Ritsos has been forced to grow. He started, as did so many writers in the twentieth century, by confronting a disintegrating culture and by responding to that disintegration with the fervour and narrowness of certainty, with a recipe for moulding existence to his own liking. Poetically, this encouraged compassionate involvement, but also a tendency towards grandiloquence and rhetorical flourish, the temptation to draw his passion larger than life-size. As his career developed, however, he learned that present vicissitudes and future hopes are but visible functions of timeless rhythms in nature, history, and human psychology. He realized more and more that the words in a poem must become 'signs for portions or classes of thought', that they must receive their meaning from what they would conceal, at the same time that they employ metaphorical power to make us see the objects and events of everyday reality. Poetically, this encouraged in him the need to register and validate existence – as opposed to the need to mould it – so that Ritsos passed from the self-absorption and self-assertion of his earliest verse to the increasing objectivity, hesitancy and reticence that we have seen as his career unfolded.

What has remained unaltered throughout all this development is Song. Ritsos's poetic personality, seen in its totality, is an organic whole, despite fluctuations of attitude or technique, because – whether his stance is moral outrage or forgiving acceptance, whether his stylistic mode is magniloquence or elliptical understatement – the original allegiance to Mother Poetry has never vacillated. This means three things: (1) unshaken faith in words: in each word as an outlet for a meeting between the reader and the poet's inner or outer world, no matter how often that meeting is postponed; (2) realization that although poetry ultimately treats universal and general classes of thought, it must do so through the senses, not the intellect, and must therefore cling to individual, palpable objects of experience, operating by means of language that is vitally metaphorical in that it establishes relationships between the single and the generic; (3) gratitude towards life in its totality – its ugliness and evil included – for providing the materials of poetry and the human consciousness which transubstantiates those materials into art. In short, what we see unchanged in Ritsos, throughout his growth, is the primal aesthetic drive: the obsession with seeing life and articulating what has been seen. This drive is so vital in him that it turns even his bitterness into affirmation. 'I mark Henry James' sentence,' Virginia Woolf wrote in her diary at the height of her own chagrin. 'Observe perpetually. Observe the oncome of age. Observe greed. Observe my own despondency . . . I insist upon spending this time to the best advantage . . .'

That is what Ritsos continues to do.

Dartmouth College   PETER BIEN
June 1973

from Testimonies A (1963)

Morning

She opened the shutters. She hung the sheets over the sill. She saw
the day.
A bird looked at her straight in the eyes. 'I am alone,' she
whispered.
'I am alive.' She entered the room. The mirror too is a window.
If I jump from it I will fall in my arms.

Unexpropriated

They came. They were looking at the ruins, the surrounding
   plots of land,
they seemed to measure something with their eyes, they tasted
the air and the light on their tongues. They liked it.
Surely they wanted to take something away from us. We
buttoned up our shirts, although it was hot,
and looked at our shoes. Then one of us
pointed with his finger to something in the distance. The others
   turned.
As they were turned, he bent discreetly,
took a handful of soil, hid it in his pocket
and moved away indifferently. When the strangers turned about
they saw a deep hole before their feet,
they moved, they looked at their watches and they left.
In the pit: a sword, a vase, a white bone.

Stones

Days come, go, without effort, no surprises.
The stones soak in the light and memory.
One makes a stone a pillow.
Another puts a stone on his clothes before swimming
to keep them from being blown away by the wind. Another uses
    a stone as his stool
or to mark something in his field, in the cemetery, in the wall, in
    the woods.

Later, after sunset, when you return home,
any pebble from the beach you place on your table
is a statuette – a small Nike or Artemis's dog,
and this one, on which a young man stood with wet feet at noon,
is a Patroklus with shady shut eyelashes.

One Night

The mansion had been shut up for years,
gradually falling apart – rails, locks, balconies; until one night
the whole second floor was suddenly lit,
its eight windows wide open, the two balcony doors open with
   no curtains.

The few passers-by stopped and looked up.
Silence. Not a soul. A square lit space. Except,
leaning against the wall, an antique mirror,
with a heavy moulding made of black carved wood, mirroring
the rotten, the converging floor boards to a fantastic depth.

Gradations of Sensation

The sun sank, pink, orange. The sea,
dark, azure green. Far out, a boat –
a black rocking mark. Someone
stood up and shouted: 'A boat, a boat.'
The others, at the coffee house, left their chairs, they looked.
There was a boat for sure. But the one who had shouted,
as if guilty now, under the stern looks of the others,
looked down and said in a low voice: 'I lied to you.'

Noon

They undressed and jumped in the sea; three o'clock in the
    afternoon;
the cool water did not at all prevent their touching. The beach
    gleamed as far as one could see,
dead, deserted, barren. The distant houses shut.
The world steamed gleaming. A horse cart
was moving out of sight at the end of the street. On the roof of
    the post-office
a flag hung at half mast. Who had died?

Cast

He could remember nothing of that summer when he closed his
    eyes
except for a golden mist and the sensation of warmth from his
    ring
and also the bare, broad, sunburnt back of a young farmer
of whom he had a quick glimpse behind the osiers – two o'clock
    in the afternoon –
as he was returning from the sea – it smelled of burned weeds all
    around.
At the same time the boat whistle and the cicadas were heard.
Statues, of course, are made much later.

Moment of Devout Concentration

They were sifting sand on the beach, they loaded the horse carts.
The sun was hot, sweat dripped. Past noon
they undressed, mounted their horses and rode into the sea,
gold and black from the burning sun and from their body hair.
   A young man
uttered a cry as his palm moved to his crotch. The others
ran towards him, lifted him up, laid him down on the sand
looking at him dumb and uncomprehending, till someone
respectfully moved his palm
and they all crossed themselves, standing around him in a circle.
The horses, soaking, golden, sniffed, their muzzles pointing far
   out towards the horizon.

Summer

He walked from one end of the beach to the other, bright
in the glory of the sun and of his youth. Every so often he'd jump
   in the sea
making his skin shine – gold, the colour of clay. Whispers of
   admiration followed him,
from men and women. A few feet behind him came
a young girl from the village, carrying his clothes devoutly,
always at some distance – she wouldn't lift her eyes to look at him
   – a little angry
and happy in her devout concentration. One day they quarrelled
and he forbade her to carry his clothes. She
threw them on the sand – she only held on to his sandals;
she put them under her armpits and disappeared running,
leaving behind her in the sun's heat a small, an awkward little
   cloud from her bare feet.

Almost a Conjurer

From a distance he lowers the light of the oil lamp, he moves the
    chairs
without touching them. He gets tired. He takes off his hat and
    fans himself.
Then, with a drawn out gesture, he produces three playing cards
from the side of his ear. He dissolves a green, pain-soothing star
in a glass of water, stirring it with a silver spoon.
He drinks the water and the spoon. He becomes transparent.
A goldfish can be seen swimming inside his chest.
Then, exhausted, he leans on the sofa and shuts his eyes.
'I have a bird in my head,' he says. 'I can't get it out.'
The shadows of two huge wings fill the room.

Audible and Inaudible

An abrupt, unexpected movement; his hand
clutched the wound to stop the blood,
although we had not heard a shot
nor a bullet flying. After a while
he lowered his hand and smiled,
but again he moved his palm slowly
to the same spot; he took out his wallet,
he paid the waiter politely and went out.
Then the little coffee cup cracked.
This at least we heard clearly.

Memory

A warm smell had remained in the armpits of her overcoat.
The overcoat on the hanger in the corridor was like a drawn
    curtain.
Whatever happened now was in another time. The light changed
    faces,
all unknown. And if someone made to enter the house,
that empty overcoat would raise its arms slowly, bitterly,
to shut the door again, silently.

The Alibi

She looked at herself in the dark window of the sidestreet
and, as she was lit on one side by the light which moved
and on the other by her bitter smile,
the deep wrinkles showed next to her eyes.
'I'm getting old,' she said; and she felt a sweet numbness in her
    limbs.
She then opened her purse to give
alms to the beggar. But there was no beggar
anywhere in the street. She noticed her gesture
reflected in the shop window – perhaps a reversal,
an innocent, gentle self-deception – even perhaps deception –
and she smiled again to her spectre. Then she took out her comb
and calmly combed her hair, surely as an alibi.
Even if there were no longer a way nearer or further away,
at least there were, deep in the shop window, her lit wrinkles
like a small upright ladder. She could climb out.
But what if, behind the pane, right behind her image,
the shop assistant was looking, invisible?

Association

He said: 'the anchor' – not in the sense of fastening down,
or in relationship to the sea-bed – nothing like this.
He carried the anchor to his room, hung it
from the ceiling like a chandelier. Now, lying down, at night,
he looked at this anchor in the middle of the ceiling knowing
that its chain continued vertically beyond the roof
holding over his head, high up, on a calm surface,
a big, dark, imposing boat, its lights out.
On the deck of this boat, a poor musician
took his violin out of its case and started playing;
while he, with an attentive smile, listened
to the melody filtered by the water and the moon.

The Somnambulist and the Other

He couldn't sleep all night. He followed
the somnambulist's steps above him on the roof. Each step
echoed without end in his own hollowness,
thick and muffled. He stood at the window, waiting
to catch him if he fell. But if he too was pulled down in his fall?
   A shadow
of a bird on the wall? A star? He? His hands?

The thud was heard on the stone pavement. Dawn.
The windows opened. The neighbours ran. The somnambulist
was running down the fire escape
to look at the one who had fallen from the window.

Shadows of Movement

'I'll go away' – she said – 'I'll go away. I can't go on; this wind . . .'

He threw down the playing cards. Steps were heard on the stairs.

The door opened. A scrap of light hit the floor.

The woman picked the playing cards off the floor and handed them back to him

with a gesture like someone returning after years.

She then went to change the water of the flowers.

But what she'd said buzzed around the room

like a fly locked in its buzzing at the beginning of winter.

Alone with His Work

He rode alone all night, frightened, mercilessly spurring
the ribs of his horse. They'll be waiting for him, it was said, to
   come without fail;
there was great need. When he arrived at dawn,
no one was waiting for him, no one was there. He looked around.
Desolate houses, locked up. They were sleeping.
He heard, next to him, his horse, panting –
foam on its mouth, wounds on its ribs and its back scratched.
He put his arms round his horse's neck and wept.
The horse's eyes, big, dark, dying,
were two towers, his own, distant, in a landscape where it
   rained.

Knocking

The salt, the sun, the water eat away the houses little by little.
One day, where there were windows and people, only wet stones
    remain
and a statue, its face in the soil. The doors, alone,
sail on the sea, stiff, unused to it, awkward. Sometimes at sunset
you see them shining on the water, flat, shut forever. Fishermen
do not look at them. They sit at early dawn in their houses before
    oil lamps,
they hear the fish slip inside their bodies' cracks,
they hear the sea knocking at them with a thousand hands (all
    unknown)
and then they go to their beds, they fall asleep with shells tangled
    in their hair.
Suddenly they hear knocking on these doors and they wake up.

from Testimonies B (1966)

Unconfirmed

He always insisted on that great gleam.
I touch it – he says – not only do I see it – I don't see it,
I touch it only, I have it, I am it. And as it grew dark
and the room, the tables, the trays became indistinct,
the sea-scapes, the grandfather clock, our faces,
he really gleamed on his chair,
his chair with its four legs also gleamed
as if resting on a cloud. We made as if
to touch him to confirm. But we did not dare
get up from our seats because we were leaning
over the top steps of a staircase without steps,
a very high staircase we had not climbed.

The Day of a Sick Man

All day, a smell of rotting, wet floor boards –
they dry and steam in the sun. The birds
glance down momentarily from the roof tops and fly away.
At night, in the neighbouring tavern, sit the grave-diggers,
they eat whitebait, they drink, they sing
a song full of black holes –
a breeze starts blowing out from the holes
and the leaves, the lights quiver, the paper lining his shelves
   quivers too.

His Find

George sits at the coffee house; he drinks his coffee; he doesn't
    look at the sea.
The farmers are gathering the grapes – their voices reach here.
The blacksmith is nailing horseshoes on a horse's hoofs in front
    of the gipsy tent.
A cart went by loaded with tomatoes.

He doesn't know what to do. The sea, of course, pale blue,
and the sun, as always, sun. The horseshoe
hanging on the door has six empty holes.

The Suspect

He locked the door. He looked suspiciously behind him
and shoved the key in his pocket. It was just then he was arrested.
They tortured him for months. Until, one evening, he confessed
(which was considered proof) that the key and the house
were his own. But no one understood
why he should try to hide the key. And so,
despite his acquittal, he remained to them a suspect.

The Same Night

When he switched on the light in his room, he knew at once
this was himself, in his own space, cut off from
the infinity of the night and from its long branches. He stood
before the mirror to confirm himself. But what about these keys
hung from his neck on a dirty string?

Spring

A glass wall. Three naked girls
sit behind it. A man
climbs up the stairs. His bare soles
appear rhythmically one after the other, dusty
with red soil. Soon
the silent, short-sighted glare covers
the whole garden and you hear
the glass wall cracking up vertically,
cut by a big, secret, invisible diamond.

Another Holiday

Everything was fine. The clouds in the sky.
The baby in the cradle. The window
in the washed water glass. The tree in the room.
The woman's apron on the chair.
The words in the poem. And only
a very shiny leaf stood out,
and the key through a feather chain.

Blowing

Opposite the window, the big sunflowers.
On the dirt road, dust from the passing horse.
She stands there still waiting. Sad.
The light reflecting on her face may be
from the sunflowers opposite. And suddenly
she flings up her arms, she chases the wind,
she grabs the rider's straw hat, clutches it to her breast,
she goes in and shuts the window.

Another Time

Big moon; silver quiet; nothing.
A white horse behind the garden railings.
They are made of light. A young man
entered the garden – he didn't open the gate,
he went right through the railings. On his chest and on his thighs
remained four broad, gold embroiderings –
the meanders from the imprints of the rails.
Under the trees the horse neighed.

Dazzled

I couldn't discern – he says – from a distance, what it was,
that bleached thing hanging about his waist. He was almost
   naked,
tanned, the colour of soil, standing next
to the upright beams, broad shouldered in a disproportionate way
for his age (I saw this when I got nearer). And that thing about
   his waist
was the white apron with the nails. I could not
greet him. I held the nails
between my teeth – in fact, they shone in the sun
and dazzled me. But I wasn't a carpenter.

Morning Rain

He saw the colours of rain behind the window panes –
the smooth yellow in the reeds, the rust on the rail,
the shadowed green in the ashen grey. He saved
the colour of transparency till last – the glass
of the water glass and the window pane. In the bathroom mirror
he saw the three naked girls. Their arms, pink,
danced behind the steam. One of them bent down
to pick up a flower. Her hair covered
her face and one breast. She raised herself up again,
she shook her hair back. Five silver drops
splashed on the mirror. She wasn't holding a flower.

Emergence

He couldn't have been more than eighteen. He took off all his
   clothes,
as if playing, but obeying something
we too could recognize. He climbed up the rock
maybe to make himself look taller. And maybe he thought
that height concealed nudity. It wasn't necessary.
Who cares about height at such moments?
There was a pink stripe about his waist –
a mark from his tight belt. He seemed
even more naked with that. And then, with a superb jump,
despite the January cold, he dived into the sea.
Soon he reappeared holding the cross up high.

The Main Thing

In spite of his insistent observations about the door,
intensely red on the blind façade, we knew
he had omitted the main thing. Opposite,
on the small hill, the man from the village came out to feed his
    horse,
he put down his bundle of straw and sat on the stone
looking quietly and a little sadly at the animal's balls.

Posture

He was standing completely naked on the beach.
The sky licked his hair.
The sea licked his feet. The sunset
tied a red ribbon crosswise on his chest,
tightened it about his waist. One end
hung down to his left knee.

Conveniences

There was nothing more to do. He accepts. The day is beautiful,
big, bright, with islands of shadows. He goes up
to the fifth floor. He observes a water glass,
fine and decisive in its transparency. He knows –
down, on the dusty sidewalk, are spilled
the black water-melon seeds, drying in the sun.
A woman is peeping through the shutters across the street.
Around her play small mobile mirrors.
One of her hands is gold, the other red.

Working-Class Beauty

He was pacing nervously up and down the dirt road, sweating, guarding
the broken-down lorry and its load. Barefoot,
his trousers rolled up, like an ancient oarsman,
with broad, tanned feet, sculptured muscles
on his bare arms. As the breeze blew
his powerful back was outlined through his shirt. The girls
returning from the beach at noon
lingered at that point of the street to tie their sandals
or tighten their belts. And then he
climbed up on his melons in the truck, took out his comb and
combed his hair.

In Foreign Parts

He looks all around. He doesn't know where he is. The sunset
noble, distant. He recognizes the garden rails,
the door knob, the windows, the cypress.
But he? A calm lake is mirrored
high up, in a cloud – a pink lake
with gold edges. Up there
he has left his shoes, his clothes. Now,
naked like this, how can he stand in the middle of the road,
naked like this, how can he enter the foreign house?

Approximately

He picks up in his hands things that don't match – a stone,
a broken roof-tile, two burned matches,
the rusty nail from the wall opposite,
the leaf that came in through the window, the drops
dropping from the watered flower pots, that bit of straw
the wind blew in your hair yesterday – he takes them
and he builds, in his backyard, approximately a tree.
Poetry is in this 'approximately'. Can you see it?

Performances

He drew the red cloth, one yard above
their chairs. He performed before their eyes
their own sufferings. He appeared nude
behind the glass partition, with the nude woman;
flashes from the five knives were also seen.
The terracotta statue crashed in the corner of the bath.
In a marine light he pulled up the big net
with the hideous hairy monster. He went up the stairs
holding a candle. He shouted down the tunnel.
He actually smashed a plate. The others,
appeased, applauded and left. He
collected the fragments of the plate and spent all night
trying to put them together. One piece
was missing right from the middle. And now he didn't have
   anything
to eat his supper from. And he wasn't even hungry.

Unreasoned

No, no – he says; perhaps everything else but not the light,
not unsupported – he says – on its own; I can't accept this;
I hold it, I pull its tail,
I pull the curtain, I smash the window pane,
I knock over the bench in the garden,
I see a small stain on your coat,
I see a layer of dust on your toe-nail,
I bury the key in your sweaty armpit,
I am a man, I tell you, I climb up the stairs two steps at a time,
I go out on the balcony and hang out the flag.

Guilt

He took his cap and went out. She
remained at the table next to the lamp. When his footsteps
became distant, she looked at her hand in the light. 'It's beautiful,'
 she said. And then,
as if justifying herself to someone there,
she took the bread to the kitchen and turned the light off.
Outside passed the carts and the moon.

Submission

She opened the window. The wind struck,
with a burst, her hair, like two big birds,
over her shoulders. She shut the window.
The two birds were on the table
looking at her. She lowered her head
between them and cried quietly.

Going Away

He vanished at the end of the road.
The moon was already high.
A bird screeched in the trees.
An ordinary, simple story.
No one took heed.
Between the two street lamps
a big blood blotch.

Exiled Twice

She arranges the flowers in the vases, she tidies up, lingers on,
hovers about the man. He's silent.
A quiet morning on the four windows. In her hand,
her feather duster flies over the furniture
with an absent-minded care. He
sees it as a richly coloured bird strutting
about the porcelain statuettes. She
stands still, hesitates, finally leans over him: 'No, no,'
'not bird,' she tells him, 'not bird,' and she weeps.

Evening

She watered the flowers. She listened to the water dripping from
   the balcony.
The planks get soaked and rot. Tomorrow,
when the balcony collapses, she will remain up in the air,
calm, beautiful, holding in her arms
the two big pots of her geraniums and her smile.

Acrobat

Muscular and well built. No geometrical shape
is foreign to his body. He bends back,
he turns about, he puts his head
between his legs; his face
smiles next to his shoes; he jumps up;
he grabs hold of his ankles in the air; he sits there
for a few seconds; he turns again. Perpetually stretched out,
his limbs seem naked. His colour changes
from pink to deep purple – a basic
colour, fleshy – it covers the shapes;
his exploit can't be seen; completely naked. Only
when he stands up and is still, he weeps.
Then we applaud, we shout, we leave.
The lights go down in the corridor. They are turned off.

About Colours

He must, he said, avoid colours. In the last resort,
only chestnut brown and ash grey with off-white spaces.
Tried tones. Seriousness. But his mouth
was deep red and a pale blue-mauve shadow
showed between his lower lip and chin.

Lightness

The sun sets A caique enters the port.
Gold and rose, steamy silence. An oar
gleams. And the purple rope ladder.
Everything light – no stone, no wood.
The silver eyebrow of the moon, refracted. Three
buttons are scarcely shining on your shirt.
And death, too, is absent from lightness.

An Old Fisherman

Now – he says – I never go fishing.
I sit here in the coffee house, I look out of the window.
The young fishermen come in with their baskets.
They sit, drink, chat. Fish
gleam differently from wine glasses. I think of telling them,
also of telling them about that big fish, the harpoon
stuck at a slant into its back; about its long shadow
on the sea bed at sunset. I didn't tell them.
They don't love dolphins. And these window panes
are dirty with brine. They need cleaning.

Leftovers

I have nothing and I can remember nothing – he said.
Season after season – faint colours,
a smell of rotting fruit, at midday,
and the whitewash dazzling. One night,
when you lit a match, I had a glimpse
of that tiny shadow that hid
under your ear. This only. The rest
is blown away already by the wind under the trees
together with paper napkins and vine leaves.

Heat

The rocks, the flaming noon, the big waves –
the sea indifferent, dangerous, strong. On the upper street,
the muleteers shout, their carts full of water-melons.
Then, a knife, the soft slit, the wind,
the red flesh and the black seeds.

Unloading

There are fewer colours now. It doesn't matter – he says.
This minimal green of the fields is enough for me.
Besides, everything diminishes with the years.
Maybe because things become concentrated and fuse. A leaf,
even when it just moves, opens a door for me,
I enter the corridor, I walk towards the end
between two rows of windows and statues –
the windows are white, the statues red.
I can clearly discern the owl, the snake, the deer.

Barbershop

They fixed up a small room among the ruins
with bricks and cardboard in the windows; they also put up a
     sign;
it read 'Barbershop'. Late, on Saturdays, around dusk,
in the dim light from the half open door, facing the sea,
the mirror pale blue – the young fishermen
and the boatmen come to shave. Then,
when it is quite dark, they go out the other door,
quiet, shadowy, with long reverent beards.

Recollection

The house was burned. Through the empty windows,
the sky. Down in the valley
the voices of the grape harvesters, remote. Later
came the three young men with pitchers,
they washed the statues with must. They ate
the figs. They undid their belts,
they sat next to one another among the dry thorns,
they tied their belts again and left.

Race of Shadows

At the summer solstice, when it was very hot,
we'd walk for hours on the sacred avenue
outside the city walls. Endless dust,
sweat and blinding sun. The white parasol
was held over the heads of the two priests
by the four offspring of Eteoboutadae,
sweating, pitiful, and still haughty. It seemed
as if the entire sun concentrated on this
moving dazzling white tent. Finally, when we arrived,
the bare stones blinding us, we covered the icon with soil. And
  then
the sweating stopped at once. A fine dew
made the parasol damp. Light clouds appeared
over the tops of the hills. A shadow came down over the eye-
  lashes.
Maybe it was from the exhaustion of this march. But no.
The youths were already undressing. The athletic games were
  starting.

First Pleasure

Proud mountains, Kallidromon, Oite, Othrys,
sovereign rocks, vines, wheat and olive groves;
They've made quarries here, the sea has pulled back;
strong smell of sun-burnt mastic trees,
the resin dripping in clots. Big
descending night. There, on the bank, Achilles,
not yet an adolescent, as he was tying his sandals,
felt that special pleasure as he held
his heel in his palm. His mind wandered for a moment
as he looked at the reflections in the water. Then
he went into the smithy to order his shield –
he knew now the shape in every detail, the scenes depicted on it,
  the size.

The Wrath

He shut his eyes to the sun. He dipped his feet in the sea. He
   noticed
the expression of his hands for the first time. A concealed
   fatigue
wide as freedom. Representatives
came and went bringing gifts and pledges,
promising titles and rich spoils. He, unconvinced,
looked at a crab staggering up a pebble
slowly, suspiciously, and yet in an official way as if ascending
   eternity.
They didn't know his wrath was only an excuse.

Necrography

When the sun went down, they carried the dead to the
    shore.
A gold, mauve and pink reflection spread far over the semi-
    circle of the damp sand. And it was strange –
this brilliance and these faces – not at all dead; especially
their bodies, young and exuberant, anointed with aromatic oils,
more suited to beds of love. Where the tents were, a radio
had been left turned on. The triumphant march
could be heard clearly down here, while the last reflection from
    the dusk
was going out, purple, on Eumelos's toe-nails and his shield.

from Testimonies C (1966–7)

Ancient Movement

Deep heat all day long. The horses sweat by the sunflowers.
A wind starts, coming from the mountain, in the afternoon. A
   sound
which is eternal, round, passes through the olive grove. Then
the hundred-year-old woman comes out into her little garden,
to her low stool under the mulberry tree near the well,
and with an ancient movement, before sitting down, she dusts
with her long, hieratic wooden arm her black apron.

Around the Well

The three women sat around the well holding their pitchers.
Big red leaves fell on their hair and shoulders.
Someone hidden behind the plane-trees threw a stone.
The pitcher broke. The water did not spill; it remained standing,
all shining, looking towards where we were hiding.

Inactivity

How we lived – he said – all these years in this house.
A furnished room. The corridor dark.
The grey, the woodworm, the icy sheets.
That man sleeping on his back on our bed
was a total stranger. The cockroaches came into
the bedrooms from the kitchen. One night
someone asked for us at the main door. The landlady
said something in the dark (surely, about us). Later
we heard again the door creaking. Neither steps nor talk.

The Decline of Narcissus

The plaster had come off the wall here and there.
His socks and shirt on the chair.
Under the bed, the same shadow, always unknown.
He stood naked before the mirror. He concentrated.
'Impossible,' he said. 'Impossible.' He took from the table
a big lettuce leaf, brought it to his mouth and started
chewing it, standing there naked before the mirror, trying
to recapture or to mimic his naturalness.

from Tanagra Women (1967)

The Potter

One day he finished with the pitchers, the flower pots, the cook-
ing pots. Some clay
was left over. He made a woman. Her breasts
were big and firm. His mind wandered. He returned home late.
His wife grumbled. He didn't answer her. Next day
he kept more clay and even more the following day.
He wouldn't go back home. His wife left him.
His eyes burn. He's half-naked. He wears a red waist-band.
He lies all night with clay women. At dawn
you can hear him sing behind the fence of the workshop.
He took off his red waist-band too. Naked. Completely naked.
  And all around him
the empty pitchers, the empty cooking pots, the empty flower
  pots
and the beautiful, blind, deaf-and-dumb women with the bitten
  breasts.

Way of Salvation

Nights; big storms. The lonely woman hears
the waves climbing up the stairs. She's afraid
they'll reach the second storey, they'll put the lamp out,
they'll soak the matches, they'll make their way to the bed. Then,
the lamp in the sea will be like the head of a drowned man
with only one yellow thought. This saves her.
She hears the waves retreat again. On the table,
she sees the lamp – its glass a little clouded by the salt.

Of the Sea

Dexterous, proud, handsome, with a strong knife,
he cut up the large fish in pieces on the wharf –
he threw the tail and the head in the sea.
The blood trickled on the boards, shining.
His feet and hands were red.
One woman told another: 'His knife
red – how well it suits his black eyes –
red, black, red –.' In the narrow street above,
the fishermen's children
weighed fish, coal
on an ancient pair of sooty scales.

Night Ritual

They killed the cock, the dove, the goat. With the blood
they covered their shoulders, their necks, their faces. One
turned to the wall and smeared his sex with blood. Then
the three women standing in a corner, covered with white veils,
uttered small cries as if being slaughtered. The men,
as if not hearing, were scribbling on the floor with a piece of
    chalk
uncoiled snakes and ancient arrows. Outside,
the drums rolled, their sound reaching the entire neighbourhood.

Face or Façade?

'I carved this statue in the stone' – he said –
'not with a hammer; with my bare fingers, with my bare eyes,
with my bare body, with my lips. Now I don't know
who is I and who's the statue.'

                    He hid behind it,
he was ugly, ugly – he embraced it, lifted it holding it around
    the waist
and they walked together.
                    And then he'd tell us that supposedly
this statue (marvellous, indeed) was he; or even
that the statue walked on its own. But who believes him?

Prisoner

Every time he opened his window, he'd see himself
through the window of the house across the street
in the long mirror in the other room, clandestine,
as if he'd entered it to steal something. Unbearable – not being
    able
to take a little air, a little sun – nothing. One day,
he took a stone, he aimed, threw it. With the noise
his neighbour appeared at his window: 'Thank God' – he
    said –
'whenever I tried to look at myself in my own mirror, yours
looked at me in a shifty way, behind my back; – unbearable.'
    The other
turned back into his room, into his own space. There, in his
    mirror
stood his neighbour, facing him, a knife between his teeth.

Inventory

At night, one wall may be divined behind the other. The deer
will not come to drink water from the fountain. They stay in the
   forests.
When there's a moon, the first wall crumbles, then the second,
then the third. The hares come down, they graze in the valley.
Everything is as it is, soft, undefined, silver,
the bull's horn in the moonlight, the owl on the roof
and the sealed crate floating down the river all on its own.

Death at Carlovassi

The dead man and the icon were in the inner room. The woman
stood over him. Both with crossed arms. She didn't recognize
   him.
She uncrossed her arms. The other woman, in the kitchen,
was cleaning the string beans. The sound of boiling water in the
   pot
poured into the dead man's room. The elder son came in. He
   looked around.
He slowly pulled off his cap. The first woman, as noiselessly as
   she could,
gathered the egg shells from the table and put them in her
   pocket.

from Stones (1968)

Unfinished

Clouds on the mountain. Who is to blame? What? Silent, tired,
he looks before him, he turns back, he walks, he bends.
The stones are down, the birds are up. A pitcher
in the window. Thistles in the valley. Hands in pockets.
Pretexts, pretexts. The poem delays. Empty.
The word is signified by what it would conceal.

from Repetitions (1968)

After the Defeat

After the destruction of the Athenians at the Aegospotami, a
    little later,
after our final defeat, free discussions, the Periclean glory,
the flourishing of the arts, the gymnasiums, the symposia of our
    philosophers have all vanished. Now
gloom, a heavy silence in the marketplace, and the impurity of
    the Thirty Tyrants.
Everything (even what is most our own) happens by default
    without
chance for appeal, defence or justification,
or even formal protest. Our papers and our books are burned,
the honour of our country rots. Even if an old friend could be
    allowed
to come as witness, he would refuse out of fear
of getting in the same trouble – he would be right of course. So,
it is better to be here – who knows, maybe we can acquire a
    fresh contact with nature,
looking at a fragment of the sea, the stones, the weeds,
or at a cloud at sunset, deep, violet, moving, behind the barbed
    wire. And maybe
a new Kimon will arrive one day, secretly led
by the same eagle, and he'll dig and find our iron spear point,
rusty, that too almost disintegrated, and he might go
to Athens and carry it in a procession of mourning or triumph
    with music and with wreaths.

And Narrating Them . . .

The way we, words, ideas have declined, we can't be bothered
with old or recent glories, with Aristides' biographies – and
    when one of us
sometimes starts reminiscing about the 300 or the 200, at once
the others cut him short with scorn, or at least sceptically. But
    sometimes, as now,
when the weather clears up – on a Sunday, sitting under a
    eucalyptus,
in this inexorable light, a secret longing comes over one
for the old glories – no matter that we call them cheap – when
    the procession started at dawn,
in front the trumpeter, behind the chariots heavy with branches
    of myrtle and wreaths,
then the black bull and young men carrying wine and milk pitchers
for the libations and beautiful oil and perfume bottles –
but what was most dazzling, at the end of the procession, dressed
    entirely in purple,
the Archon of Plateae who the rest of the year was not permitted
to touch iron and had to dress entirely in white, now dressed in
    purple,
carrying a long sword, crossing the town majestically,
towards the heroes' graves, holding a pitcher from the state
    utensils, and
after the gravestones had been washed, after the rich sacrifices,
    he'd raise
the cup of wine and pouring it over the tombs recite:
'I am offering this cup to the bravest men who fell
for the freedom of the Greeks,' – and a shiver would pass
through the nearby laurel woods,
a shiver which still flutters through the leaves of these eucalyptuses
and through these patched clothes all different colours hung in
    the sun to dry.

124

The New Dance

Not only excuses, but genuine motives, important consequences –
passions, interests, dangers, fears – Pasiphae, the Minotaur,
the Labyrinth and Ariadne, her beautiful erotic thread
unwinding, guiding him in the stone darkness. Then
Theseus' triumphant return. He stopped at Delos
and there Theseus danced around the Keraton (the famous altar
     made entirely of horns)
together with the youths from Athens that accompanied him,
     a new
extraordinary dance with criss-crossing steps that repeated
     perhaps,
in the strong noon light, the dark turns of the Labyrinth and,
     perhaps
who knows what – the birds and the cicadas made so much noise
     in the small nearby pine forest –
you couldn't make it out, you were dizzy from the sun and the
     reflections from the sea,
a fine powdered glass, and the dazzling movements of the naked
     bodies –
an extraordinary dance. And later we forgot all about
Minotaurs, Pasiphaes and Labyrinths and even poor Ariadne
dying abandoned all alone on Naxos. But the dance
quickly spread in the country and we still dance it. Ever since,
the palm wreath has been decreed the trophy
at the athletic Delian gymnic games.

The Decline of the Argo

Tonight talking of how things pass, age, become cheap –
beautiful women, exploits, poems – we remembered
the legendary ship when it was brought to Corinth one spring
   night,
eaten by woodworm, fading, its tholepins torn off,
full of patches, holes, memories. The long procession through
   the woods,
with torches, wreaths, flutes, contests of youths. The old Argo
   was
a magnificent offering to Poseidon's temple. Beautiful night; the
   chanting of the priests;
an owl hooting from the temple's pediment; the dancers would
   jump lightly
on the ship imitating rough action with improper grace, the
   motion
of non-existent oars, sweat, blood. Then an old sailor
spat at his feet and walked away to the small woods to piss.

Penelope's Despair

Not that she didn't recognize him in the dim light of the fire,
his disguise in beggar's rags. No. There were clear signs:
the scar on the knee-cap, his muscular body, the cunning look.
  Frightened,
leaning against the wall, she tried to find some excuse, a delay to
  avoid answering
so as not to betray her thoughts. Was it for him she had wasted
  twenty years
waiting and dreaming? Was it for this wretched stranger
soaked in blood, with his white beard? She fell speechless on a
  chair,
she looked closely at the slaughtered suitors on the floor as if
  looking
at her own dead desires and she said 'welcome',
her voice sounding to her as if it came from a distance, as if some-
  one else's. The loom in the corner
cast shadows across the ceiling like a cage, the birds she had
  woven
with bright red threads among green leaves suddenly
turned grey and black
flying low on the flat sky of her final endurance.

from Railings (1969)

The Armchair

This armchair was where the dead man sat. The green velvet
is shiny where his arms rested. After, when he was taken away,
the flies came – some quiet enormous flies. It was winter.
Big orange crop – they'd throw oranges away behind the fences
   of storage yards;
it was also cloudy – you couldn't tell when it dawned. One day,
early in the morning, the decorators knocked on the door with
   their brushes.
The thin servant answered. He gave them the dead man's ties –
a pale blue one, a yellow one, a black one. They winked at him.
   They left.
The armchair is in the basement, the mouse trap on it.

Reconstruction of Sleep

At night, big chunks of plaster fell from the ceiling onto the bed.
There was nowhere to lie down. The mirror too had shattered.
The plaster statue in the corridor was covered with soot – you couldn't
even touch it, let alone make love to it – black marks
were left on the thighs, the knees, the lips, the palms. It had been months
since the water, the telephone, the electricity were cut off. On the marble-topped table
in the kitchen, next to the cigarette butts, two huge lettuces were rotting.

These

Huge trucks speed past on the highway at night
loaded with drums of barbed wire and gas masks.
At dawn, below the stone building, they crank the motorcycles.
A very pale man, wearing a red tunic, comes out on the roof,
looks at the shut windows, the hills, he points a thin finger,
one by one he counts the holes in the dove-cot abandoned long
   ago.

Search

Come in, Gentlemen – he said. No inconvenience. Look through
  everything;
I have nothing to hide. Here's the bedroom, here the study,
here the dining-room. Here? – the attic for old things; –
everything wears out, Gentlemen; it's full; everything wears out,
  wears out,
so quickly too, Gentlemen; this? – a thimble; – mother's;
this? mother's oil-lamp, mother's umbrella – she loved me
  enormously; –
but this forged identity card? this jewellery, somebody else's? the
  dirty towel?
this theatre ticket? the shirt with holes? blood stains?
and this photograph? his, yes, wearing a woman's hat covered
  with flowers,
inscribed to a stranger – his handwriting –
who planted these in here? who planted these in here? who
  planted these in here?

Interrogation Offices

Long corridor. Shut doors on both sides.
Chimney of an invisible stove – it smoked a little. At the other
   end,
five men dressed in black, wearing identical masks, looked at
   him.
He knocked at one door. Nothing. At the second, the third, to
   the end.
No answer. And then again down the other side, knock after
   knock,
at all the doors. Nothing. The masked men not moving.
So? As he made to pass through the doorway and go away,
the door shut by itself. It got dark. It was raining outside.
He heard the water on the tin roof, on the tiles in the courtyard.
   He just had time
to fix in his memory: – the wet asphalt reflecting
the new barbershop made of glass, with high pale blue armchairs.

Not at all Little

Something more; – what? He doesn't know himself. Add.
Add it to what? Make it what? He doesn't know. He doesn't
  know.
Only this will – his own. He takes a cigarette. He lights it.
It is windy out. The palm trees in the church-yard will be torn
  down. The wind
does not enter the clocks. Time is not shaken. Nine, ten,
eleven, twelve, one. They are setting the table in the room next
  door,
they're bringing the plates. The old woman crosses herself. The
  spoon
moves to the mouth. A slice of bread is under the table.

The Girl Who Found Her Sight

Ah – she says – I see again. There. All these years my eyes were
    strangers to me,
they'd sunk in me; they were two mouldy pebbles
in dark, thick water – black water. Now –
isn't that a cloud? and this a rose? – tell me;
and this a leaf – isn't it green? – g-r-e-e –
and this, my voice – yes? – and can you hear me talk?
Voice and eyes – isn't this what's called freedom?
Down in the basement I've forgotten the broad silver tray,
the cardboard boxes, the cages and the spools of string.

from Gestures (1969–70)

In the Dark

The lamplighter went by at sunset with his ladder,
he lit the lamps of the island as if drilling holes in the darkness,
as if drilling big yellow wells. In the wells
the lamps, upright, swayed, copper-green, drowned;
a cross flashed on the belfry of Saint Pelagia;
a dog barked behind the stable, another at the Customs;
the tavern sign dripped blood; the man, barechested,
held a big red knife; the woman,
uncombed, beat the eggwhites in a bowl.

At Least the Wind

Night. Dining-room. Flies on the chandelier;
flies in the tray, on the bread, on the glasses. The old man
chews greedily; he spies on the other plates.
White tablecloth, very white. The wind
in the street with the street lamps. Ah the wind
with its long, humming, shiny tubes
secretly inserted in the walls, under the table,
in the springs of big beds, sucking
flies, paper napkins, sleep. Ah the wind – he said.
He put his spoon down; he went out. We'd
wait all night for his return
dropping now and then
small square ice cubes
in the carafe.

Indisposition

He was almost sick next morning.
He was pumped with words last night.
He can't bear words; he can't shake them off.
They're painting sheer white the house across the street,
indecently white. The voices of the decorators sound
very loud in the winter light. One
on the roof-top has embraced the chimney
as if fucking it. Thick drops of whitewash
splash on the black soil with the rotten leaves.

Before Sleep

She tidied up, she washed the plates.
Everything is quiet. Eleven o'clock.
She took off her shoes to go to bed.
She delays. She lingers at the side of her bed.
Has she forgotten something that her day does not want to end?
– The house, then, is not square, nor the bed, nor the table. –
Unconsciously she lifts her stocking before the lamp
to find the hole. She sees nothing. Yet she is certain it is there
– maybe in the wall, or in the mirror; –
it's through this hole she hears the night snort.
The shadow of the stocking on the sheet is a net
in cold water crossed by a blind yellow fish.

Enumeration

People stop in the street, they look.
The numbers over the doors mean nothing.
The carpenter is hammering a nail into a long narrow table.
Somebody sticks a list of names on the telegraph pole.
A piece of newspaper rustles, caught in the thorns.
The spiders are under the vineleaves.
A woman got out of one house to enter another.
The wall yellow and wet, its paint peeling off.
A cage with a canary in the dead man's window.

Dissolution

Sometimes words come almost by themselves, like leaves of
  trees —
the invisible roots, the soil, the sun, the water have helped,
old rotten leaves have also helped.
Meanings can easily be attached like spider webs on leaves, or
dust and drops of dew sparkling with wavering flashes.
Under the leaves, a young girl is disembowelling her nude doll;
a drop falls on her hair; she lifts her head; she sees nothing;
only the cold transparency of the drop is dissolved over her body.

The Third One

The three of them sat before the window looking at the sea.
One talked about the sea. The second listened. The third
neither spoke nor listened; he was deep in the sea; he floated.
Behind the window panes, his movements were slow, clear
in the thin pale blue. He was exploring a sunken ship.
He rang the dead bell for the watch; fine bubbles
rose bursting with a soft sound – suddenly,
'Did he drown?' asked one; the other said: 'He drowned.' The
    third one
looked at them helpless from the bottom of the sea, the way one
    looks at drowned people.

Inside and Outside the Window

Outside, big sunbathed clouds; the shadow of the church in the
    valley.
The bread folded in a napkin hanging from the tree. The wind
blows from the mountains, it burrows into small labyrinths
    under the staircase.
The woman near the window is knitting a woollen vest. The
    man
takes off his boots; he looks at his feet – his bare feet which step
    on soil. The woman
puts aside her knitting needles; she gets up; she hesitates; she
    takes the boots;
she puts her hands in them, she kneels, she crawls under the bed.

Reversal

Roots in the air; – two faces between them;
the well was at the bottom of the garden – that's where
they had thrown their rings one day; then
they looked up, very high up, pretending not to see
the old woman shitting in the empty flowerpot
as she bit into the big apple.

Awaiting His Execution

There, stood against the wall, at dawn, his eyes uncovered,
as twelve guns aimed at him, he calmly feels
that he is young and handsome, that he deserves to be clean
    shaven,
that the pale pink distant horizon becomes him –
and, yes, that his genitals retain their proper weight,
somewhat sad in their warmth – that's where the eunuchs look,
that's where they aim; – has he already become the statue of him-
    self?
Himself looking at it, all nude, on a bright day
of the Greek summer, in the square above – looking at it standing
    upright
himself behind the shoulders of the crowd, behind the hurrying
    gluttonous tourist women,
behind the three made-up old women wearing black hats.

White Landscape

He left unnoticed. Not a step was heard at the door.
It was incredible it didn't rain at all at night.
The next day endless winter sunshine,
like someone shaving in a white bathroom
before a mirror wiped by an invisible hand
with a soft, wet piece of paper, the razor dull,
skin turning red, beard left in patches,
and then that disconcerting smell of eau-de-Cologne.

Departures, III

Slowly things empty, like those big bones
one finds on the beach in summer – horse bones
or bones of prehistoric animals; they are empty of the stuff inside,
the marrow;
all that remains is a solid white, a lack of colour, with invisible
holes,
like the colour rooms take in winter when
it rains violently. You hold the doorknob, or the handle
of a tea cup and you can't tell whether you hold them or they
hold you
or whether they, or you, can be held. And suddenly as you are
about to drink your tea,
you see between your fingers the porcelain handle
by itself; – the cup is missing – you examine it: so white,
so weightless, almost bone – you think it beautiful, shaped like
a half zero – it longs to be complete, while, across, in the wall,
out of a deep crack, seeps the warm steam from the tea you did
not drink.

Circle

The same voice, still hoarser now, told him panting,
'This is where I end, this is where I begin again' – always the
   same,
a recurring circle, and in the circle
the empty bed or the bare table with the lamp
lighting two hands aimlessly moving
removing two long elastic black gloves.

A Three Storey House with Basement

On the third floor lived the eight poor students.
On the second the five seamstresses with their two dogs.
On the first the landlord with his adopted daughter.
In the basement the baskets, the jugs, the rats.
The three floors used the same staircase.
The mice went up the wall.
At night, when the train passed, the rats
went on the roof through the chimney and looked
at the sky, the clouds, the garden railings,
the lights of the restaurants,
while the eldest seamstress shut the shutters,
her mouth full of pins.

from Corridor and Stairs (1970)

Athens 1970

In these streets
people walk; people
hurry, they are in a hurry
to go away, to get away (from what?),
to get (where?) – I don't know – not faces –
vacuum cleaners, boots, boxes –
they hurry.

In these streets, another time,
they had passed with huge flags,
they had a voice (I remember, I heard it),
an audible voice.

Now,
they walk, they run, they hurry,
motionless in their hurry –
the train comes, they board, they jostle;
green, red light;
the doorman behind the glass partition;
the whore, the soldier, the butcher;
the wall is grey,
higher than time.

Even the statues can't see.

Inevitable

In the back street, on the other side, where the fire-escapes are,
where there are broken flower pots, broken carafes,
where there are dead dogs, worms, green flies,
where the ironmongers piss, the butchers, the turners –
children are scared at night; the stars shout too much,
they call from very far off as if everyone were away; –
don't talk to me again about the statues – he said; I can't stand it,
  I tell you;
no more excuses; – down in the big cellar,
lean women with long arms collect the soot from the boilers,
they paint their eyes, their teeth, the kitchen door, the carafe,
thinking they become invisible, or at least unrecognizable,
while the mirror in the corridor, skeletal, advances upon them
when they come in or go out secretly, close to the wall,
and the searchlights aim at them in the middle of the yellow
  grass.

In the Void

Water falling on stone,
the sound of water
in the winter sun,
cry of a lonely bird
in the hollow sky
searching for us again,
implying
(what 'yes' implying?)
falling
from high up
on parked buses
filled with tourists centuries dead.

Indiscreetly

Behind the ancient wall,
through the bunkers,
through the holes from dislodged stones,
the dead
with wild, dilated eyes
observed
the young hunter who pissed
on a broken capital of a column.

So, then, if life lies
death too lies.

Panorama

Rows of almond trees,
rows of statues,
high snow covered mountains,
graves,
hunters' shots in the olive grove –

Fine beauty, fine futility,
like sisters, contradicting
one another, contradicting
all the futility
of life, of death.

The hearse passed loaded
with almond blossoms.
And the statues looked out
through the windows.

The Essentials

He sews the buttons on his coat awkwardly,
with a thick needle, with thick thread.
He talks to himself:

Did you eat your bread? Did you sleep well?
Were you able to talk, to stretch your arm?
Did you remember to look out of the window?
Did you smile when you heard knocking on the door?

If it's always Death – he comes second.
Freedom always comes first.

Conscious

No, no – he says again. No, no.
He turns his clothes inside out,
he turns his glass upside down,
he turns the water inside out, he turns death inside out,
he wears his shoes on his hands,
he wears his gloves on his feet.
'You are a liar,' they tell him. They get angry.
The three women laugh on the balcony.
He does not answer. He remains motionless.
A fly sits on his cheek.
The three women laugh on the balcony.
They are young. They rustle. That's what he wants.

Desertion

Dental surgeries have multiplied in our poor suburb,
so have chemists, coffin makers. The evenings
are green light bulbs over doors whose paint is peeling,
long stripes of light. A tap
has been forgotten running all night at Crow's sidestreet
in front of the flowershop, the barbershop. Someone
is wiping his shoes before the door taking a long time
as if about to enter an empty hall
with bright waxed marble floors,
the space is unfamiliar,
equally unfamiliar the steps he takes, the movement,
the lack of windows, the silence, the key, the handkerchief.

Piraeus Detainees' Transport Section

Half a blanket under, half over; fever; cement; damp;
sweaty hair; inscriptions on the walls scratched with finger-
   nails –
names, dates, small covenants; the same nightmare
opening holes with the same torch: 'tonight', 'tonight',
'at dawn, tomorrow'. Who will be left here to remember us
when the key is heard in the lock and the long chain
is dragged on the endless white where, on one side,
the last cigarette we'd thrown down still smokes.

After the Trial

The frightened face locked. Hair ruffled;
shirt torn; bruised flesh. They gave him back
the leather belt, the wrist-watch, the black comb
left on the long table. He took them. He didn't know
what to put on – the watch? the belt? – where should he put the
    comb?
He looked at his identity card. 'Lucas,' he said;
'Lucas,' he said again to himself – he didn't raise his eyes;
he put on his watch in slow hurry (it's the fault of the table –
too bare, dark – one of its corners scratched),
he put the belt on too – tightened it. He was still tightening it
when he went out in the corridor – the old toilet stank,
the water-pipes dripped; the boy was collecting the bottles at the
    coffee-house;
the guards' voices could be heard down the light-well. 'Lucas,
    Lucas,' he said again
as if talking to a stranger in a foreign language. It was night.
The lights came on in the avenue and in the Museum Garden.

Precautions

Maybe you should still control your voice; –
tomorrow, the day after, some time,
when the others shout under the flags,
you too must shout,
but make sure you lower your cap over your eyes
low, very low,
so that they will not see where your eyes look,
no matter that you know that those who shout
look nowhere.

The Meaning Is One

Experienced words, dense, determined,
vague, insistent, simple, suspicious –
useless memories, pretexts, pretexts,
emphasis on modesty, – stones supposedly,
residences supposedly, weapons supposedly – door handle,
pitcher handle, table with vase,
made bed – smoke. Words –
you hammer them on air, on wood, on marble,
you hammer them on paper – nothing; death.

You must tighten your tie. Like this.
Keep quiet. Wait. Like this. Like this.
Slowly, slowly, in the narrow opening, there
behind the stairs, pushed against the wall.

Scene

In the corridor stood the sad woman, the lawyer, the guard.
On the floor the blankets tied up with rope. In the office next
   door
the telephone was ringing. 'At four' – they said – 'the boat.'
'At four' – they said – 'sharp.' The steel door creaked again.
They were bringing more of them into the courtyard. 'I will
   send you cigarettes,'
said the woman. 'Finish,' said the guard. On the wall
crept a big spider. The second door
opened suddenly; – the dead man fell on his face. The other
grabbed the spider, put it in his mouth; he laughed
with jaws shut tight. 'Speak,' they shouted at him. 'Speak.'
'Speak,' they threatened him. He wouldn't say a word. He
   laughed. The woman
sat on the blankets and hid her face in her hands.

from Papermade (1971)

from Papermade

In the mirror
in the right hand corner
on the yellow table
I've left the keys.
Take them.
The crystal doesn't open,
Doesn't open.

*

Landscapes race
past the train window panes.
I've found a toothpick
in my pocket,
the belfry
in my hat.

*

Roses on the trunk.
Your hand on the belt.
What did you want to ask?

*

Covered with the sheet –
how lightly she breathes –
(is it poetry?)
The boat takes off.
The sail swells.
I touch with one finger
the wind one by one
silence one by one.

*

I'll paint my shadow blue.
I'll brush my teeth
and I'll play the guitar.
You hide under the bed.
I'll pretend I don't know.

*

You keep expecting
I'll say:
'It isn't like this.'
This is how it is.
For me too.
Careful when you clip your nails.
The scissors gleam.

*

Loud wind.
Night.
The lights flicker at the harbour.
In the corridor of the customs house
the cleaning woman
sweeps quietly.
The suitcases are shut.
The sign: 'Forbidden'.
The wind a comrade.
The sails, the big sails.

          *

This light
the only one
high up on the mountain
was carried there by the dead.
Don't you remember it?

          *

And the marble
so bare
so white
not waiting for the statue.

          *

Everything is secret –
the shadow of the stone
the bird's claw
the spool of thread
the chair
the poem.

*

This nausea
is not an illness.
It is an answer.

*

They are beautiful (do you remember them?)
They walked straight.
They saw straight.
They sang.
They held their spears upright
high, high.
They didn't see
there were no flags.

*

In the wild wind
high, high,
from the height of the whitest gull –
freedom.

176

from Muffled (1972)

Secret Guilt

Sin and saintliness, we said, are the same in the same night.
The other one had sworn not to tell. But, who knows –
you can never be sure if and how long he'll keep silent,
you will keep silent; – and maybe you will rush foolishly
to anticipate the other one, looking at the rain trickling down
the illuminated panes of the restaurant, when in the crowd
the chair is heard falling, the glass breaking,
and He, with a stab in the cheek, red eyes,
stretches his huge, muscular arm and points at you.

The Poet's Profession

In the corridor, the umbrellas, the galoshes, the mirror;
in the mirror, the window a little quieter;
in the window, the gate of the hospital across the street. There,
a long queue of impatient, familiar blood-donors –
the first ones have already pulled up their sleeves
while in the inner rooms the five casualties are dead.

Concentration Camp

The whistle, the cry, the swishing, the thud;
the reversed water, the smoke, the stone, the saw;
a fallen tree among the killed men; –
when the guards undressed them, you could hear falling
one by one from their pockets the telephone tokens,
the small pair of scissors, the nail-clipper, the little mirror
and the long, hollow wig of the bald hero
strewn with straw, broken glass and thorns
and a cigarette-butt hidden behind the ear.

The Unexpressed

The city all lit up under its evening sky;
two bright red lights blink inexplicably high up;
the windows, the bridge, the streets, the taxis, the buses.
'I too had a bicycle' – he said; – 'I was dreaming' – he said.
The woman in the room looked away; she didn't say a word;
her dress was unstitched on the right side; if she stood
one could see her shoulder was bent. As for the rest,
one can't talk about them – he said; you keep them like broken
    water glasses;
you take them down yourself, when the rubbish collector passes,
with a guilty eagerness, early in the morning, the beautiful water
    glasses
wrapped in old newspapers, always anxious
you might knock them against the rails of the staircase, because
    they still ring
with a deep sound, penetrating – that unbreakable sound
as if conspiring with the window panes, with the wind, with the
    walls.
The blind musician then goes up the stairs exhausted; he puts
    down
his violin case on the chair; he opens it; in it
are two of the three water glasses, glittering, whole.

Wounded or Dead?

They took the stretcher out secretly through the back door. We
were looking through the slats of the shutters. One of them went
  back –
he must have forgotten something – maybe his comb. In the
  street
the sheet gleamed all the whiter. The lights hadn't been turned
  on yet.
I wonder if they'll have time – he said. The one with the cigarette
  which had gone out:
I – he said – why should they hide him? The woman bent down
  next to him;
her thighs showed all the way up. From the opposite side,
the big dog was approaching, holding in its teeth the mask
which was identical to the face of the one lying on the stretcher.
  And suddenly
the five strong lamps came on. Underneath, motionless,
the five informers wearing new black hats. We
moved away quickly from the slats of the shutters. The room was
  all lit
with lines and stripes – underlinings under invisible errors,
and on the table, the jewellery case, the keys and one of his shoes.

The Necessary Exclamation

You must fix the approximate time, the light, the colour;
at night when the horse-cab passes loaded with barrels,
one of its wheels crushes the pieces of plaster;
the joints of the wall creak. Behind the window panes
you can see opposite the white kitchen, the refrigerator,
the bare feet of the old man. Then, the bathroom light
goes on. They pull the curtain. The maid
takes a bowl of apples out on the balcony.
The gramophone is playing. You can't choose
between things with no relationship or contrast,
until the scream is heard and the knife is pushed into
the wooden table stabbing a paper napkin
with a perfect imprint of two painted lips.

The Dead House (1959)

The Dead House

Imaginary and authentic story of a very ancient Greek family

(Only two sisters remained of the family. One had been mad.
She imagined their house had moved to ancient Thebes, or
rather Argos – she confused mythology, history and her private
life, the past and the present, but not the future. That's all. Later
she recovered. It was she who talked to me the evening I brought
them a message from their uncle abroad – their father's brother.
The other sister didn't appear at all. But every so often she could
be heard shuffling about in her slippers in the next room while
the elder one talked):

Now, we, the two younger sisters, shuffle about all alone in this
    vast house –
so-called young – we've been old for years,
we were the youngest in the family – and, besides, the only ones
    left. We don't know
how to manage this house, how to settle down;
we can't bear to sell it – we've spent a whole life in here –
and this is the place of our dead – you can't sell them –
who will buy the dead anyhow? But, then, having to drag them
from house to house, from neighbourhood to neighbourhood –
it would be exhausting and risky – they've settled down in here,
one in the shadow of the curtain, another under the table,
another behind the wardrobe or behind the glass doors of the
    bookshelves,
another in the glass of the lamp – as modest and satisfied with so
    little as always,
another smiling discreetly behind the shadow of
my sister's knitting needles casting an X on the wall.

We've stored the heavy furniture on the floor below,
also the heavy carpets and the velvet and silk curtains,

187

tablecloths, embroidered napkins, crystal, china,
big silver trays which used to mirror the broad face of hospitality,
blankets, silk eiderdowns and linen,
woollens, purses, overcoats,
ours and those of the dead – all mixed up together –
gloves, lace and ostrich feathers from mother's hats,
the piano, the guitars, the flutes, the drums,
the hobby-horses and dolls from our childhood,
father's formal uniforms and our eldest brother's first long
    trousers,
the mother-of-pearl case with the blond locks of the youngest,
    the gold inlaid knife,
riding costumes and rucksacks and cloaks – all mixed up,
without mothballs or twigs of lavender in little twill bags.

We've nailed up the rooms. We've only kept
these two rooms on the upper floor facing west,
the corridor and the staircase
for getting to the garden at night for a walk sometimes
or to go out for some quick shopping.

And even so we've got quite settled down. Of course we've got
    rid
of unnecessary movements, pointless tidying, senseless efforts
for an order impossible to give. And yet
the house, bare and closed up, has developed
a terrible, very delicate way of resounding
every time a mouse, a cockroach or a bat moves.

Every shadow deep in the mirror, every grinding
of the fine teeth of woodworm or moths,
extends infinitely up to the finest fibrous vessels of the silence,
    reaches deep into the blood-vessels
of the most improbable delusions. You can hear clearly

the drumming of the looms of the smallest spider in the basement,
    among the jars,
or the rust sawing into the handles of the cutlery
and suddenly a big thump in the lower entrance hall
when a piece of disintegrating felt peels off and falls
as when a loved old building collapses.

And when sometimes, at dawn, the dustman collects the rubbish
    in a far away neighbourhood,
his distant bell resounds on all the glass and metal,
on the bronze rails of the beds, on the ancestral portraits,
on the little bells of the pierrot costume our little brother had
    worn
on a beautiful carnival night – and we were frightened on our
    way back home,
dogs barked at us, my dress got caught in the fence,
I ran to catch up with the others; the moon stuck its face
so tightly on my face – I couldn't walk any further
and the others called me from behind the trees
and I could hear, in a different space, the glass beads of the fancy
    costumes
and the glass tassels of the stars far beyond over the invisible
    Myrtoan Sea,
and when I finally reached them, they all looked at me with
    surprise
because my face was shining, tinted with gold-dust
like the gold-dust used to paint the old chandeliers in the dining-
    room
or the living-room mirrors with their elegant, intricately carved
    consoles –

We've stored those too in the lower rooms. Of course, we could
    have
kept a few of these things for our own use,
a rocking chair, a mirror

for combing our hair sometimes. But who would look after
   them? Now
maybe we can hear them wear away, but at least we don't see
   them. Everything has abandoned us.

And these two rooms we've kept,
the coldest, the barest, the highest, and perhaps
best for looking at things from above
and from some distance, so as to feel
that we overlook and command our fate; especially
at dusk when all things bend towards the warm earth,
there's a shivering cold here sharp as a sword
for cutting off any desire for new conventions, or any hope
for an unfulfilled meeting; it is sort of healthy
in this disdainful, clean coldness.
And these two rooms hang in the boundless night
like two extinguished lanterns on a completely deserted beach,
only the lightning lights them for a few seconds and then
   extinguishes them,
it pierces and transfixes them transparent in the void, these also
   void.

But if someone happens to be strolling on the thorn-covered hill
   opposite,
late, when the sun sinks and everything is pale, blurred, violet,
when things look lost and everything seems possible, then
the lonely stroller on the hill
looks gentle, sympathetic, someone who could
still feel a little sympathy for us; – the hill then also looks
peaceful, on the same level as our window, so much so
that if the stroller were to turn in this direction to look at the
   cypress trees
you'd think that he'd cross our fence if he took one more step,
he'd enter the room like an old friend and I would even say he'd
ask for a brush to dust his shoes. But he
soon disappears behind the hill

and all that's left again across from our windows
is the curve of the hill silent like penitence
and the bitter compromised dusk that lowers itself in the
    shadows.

We're not entirely used to it – what can you do? – everything
    has abandoned us –
we have abandoned everything – a balance
is regained, an almost just balance, without mutual resentment,
without guilt and even without sadness, – how could it be other-
    wise?

We are left here now, as when you pick flowers in the garden at
    sunset,
many flowers for the dining-room vases and for the bedrooms of
    the dead,
and your hands are stained yellow with pollen,
and the road-dust which comes in through the garden rails and
    powders the stalks,
and a few little bugs, some winged, some wingless,
and the few lukewarm dewdrops,
together with those inevitable diaphanously fine cobwebs
that always stick to flowers, and as the pink dusk burns out on the
    window panes
you feel the sharp knife made blunt
by the flowers' blood and milk – a strange rich feeling
of fear and murder – a blind, a noble, fragrant, boundless beauty,
a bare absence. That's how it is. Everything has abandoned us.

On that last day, the maids shrieked and ran –
a piercing shriek that remained nailed in the dark corridor
like a big fishbone in the throat of an unknown guest
or like a rusty sword in the long coffin of the killed man,
a shriek – just that – and they left running,
faces locked in palms; only when they reached
the edge of the marble stairs, behind the peristyle,

you could see them, black, shrunk, humped,
infinitely cautious and opportunistic,
scheming, resentful, with purposeful and calculated willingness
– they stopped briefly, strangers to their shriek,
uncovered their faces,
examined carefully the stairs so as not to trip
although their feet had learned each step by heart,
they knew the staircase in all its length, with all its pauses
like a poem written on the reverse page of a calendar,
or like a song sung by soldiers after a battle
taught by the few soldiers returning from the front –

a few soldiers, still handsome, maybe a little sad,
with big feet and hands, lice in their undershirts,
underground tunnels and collapsed stars in their eyes,
eyelashes shaped like hooks, dark milky blue, like a castle's
    shadow on the fountain,
something hard and impatient on their mouths,
something very masculine and also indifferent, as if they'd kissed
many killed men on their crossed hands or on their foreheads,
as if they had abandoned their wounded comrades, running into
    the gorge under sleet,
and most of all as if they'd stolen the flask the sick man used as
    pillow. Yet,

the soldiers would sing in the kitchen at night (we were young
    then,
we'd listen to them behind closed doors – they wouldn't let us
enter the kitchens full of strange unfamiliar objects,
mysterious smells from pepper, garlic, celery, tomatoes,
and other complex smells of hidden origin,
sibylline voices of the fire, the smoke, boiling water,
the criss-crossing sound of quick knives,
the dangerous towers of unwashed plates
and the big, bare, bloody bones of mythical animals.

That was the kingdom of the maids with their suggestive aprons
in the alchemy of vegetables, meats, fruits, fishbones,
arcane witches with immense wooden ladles,
pronouncing oracles over the steam from the pots,
moulding out of smoke a delicate slaughtered woman wearing a
    white cloak
or boats with three masts and ropes, swearwords and sailors,
or shaping the long beard of a transparent blind man holding a
    lyre on his knees –
perhaps that's why mother wouldn't let us go in there;
and sometimes we'd find a handful of salt behind a door,
or a rooster's head, its comb a minute sunset, on a broken roof
    tile.

We'd say nothing to the grown-ups, because when the kitchen
    door opened a crack,
the ghost of smoke would slide out sideways, shoulder first, to
    stand for hours in the corridor,
tall, threatening, with a glass helmet with a horse tail; the ghost
lonely, fragrant, beastly, bodyless,
with no bones, yet omnipotent. So, we'd listen
behind the doors until midnight,
until we fell into a red sparkling sleep.) So, the soldiers sang,

they'd joke with the maids,
they'd pull off their boots and rub their thick toes with their
    hands
and then they'd wipe the wine off their fleshy lips
or they'd scratch their hairy chests, their crotches,
they'd grab the women's breasts
and they'd sing again (we could hear them in our sleep), they'd
    sing,

their faces hidden behind greasy hair,
imperceptibly tapping the rhythm on the tiles with their bare
    feet,

or with their fingers on a jug or on a glass,
or on the wooden table (which was for chopping meat),
softly, so softly (so that the masters would not hear);
their Adam's apples moving up and down,
a knot on a thick rope pulled from both ends,
a knot on the rope pulled out of a deep well,
a knot in the guts. And the women

hearing them would cry hysterically,
they'd rip off their clothes till they were naked, they'd plead
    with them,
they'd take them on their laps like sick children who must be
    cuddled,
they'd crave to put them whole inside their bellies
– maybe to fill up their own emptiness,
their own wombs – to keep them in
deep, deep, to drown them
to protect them, to be the only ones to
keep them – and then give birth to them

in better days, in a whiter house,
in an airier house, sunnier, with fewer shadows
from columns, jars, murders, glories, coffins, swords,
with fewer invisible holes in the walls, – holes
made from nails for hanging steel mirrors, formal dresses,
from nails for hanging uniforms, trumpets, drums, helmets,
    shields,
or for the strings of unspoken toys of dead children,
or the ikons, the wedding wreaths, the pots; holes that are
    covered up of course
by repairs, fresh whitewashing and plastering,
but that always open deeper, deeper still, in memory.

That's how they wanted to give birth to them, in a wider space
with more light, in a more solid space, in a space that isn't
    hollow

with crypts, catacombs, tombs,
in a house without locked doors behind which
you hear whispers, sobs, the terrible sound
of a woman's hair cascading to her knees, the sound of a shoe
    that's dropped far from the bed; finally

in a space of strange loneliness, sincerity and security,
in a Spring countryside, amidst young barley,
next to a red horse and an ashen, tame little donkey,
next to a dog, a cow, two sheep,
in the sole shadow of a plough. But the soldiers

neither heard, nor saw, nor felt,
brave and indifferent, drunk with death,
drowned in their own song – a song
not at all heroic, neither sad, nor crippled –
a song they'd surely been taught by their village women,
and now, returning from the front,
were teaching to the younger women. This staircase then,

the maids knew it well, like the song they'd learned again,
with all its pauses, its intervals, its dimensions,
with all the stressed and unstressed slabs,
the central incision of the landing; a thousand times they went
    up and down
in other days, happy days,
when they carried the baking trays from the baker
or the big jugs of wine from the cellars
or the big loaves of bread and the meat and the fruit
or bunches of roses, carnations, daisies
or the modest olive branches and the laurels gleaming with
    morning dew –

in other days, weddings, christenings, celebrations, birthdays,
on days of triumph and glory, when the messenger, covered in
    dust

would fall down panting on these stairs
kissing the marble, crying,
announcing in a deep and somewhat hoarse voice,
strange in the lapping of his final sobs;

and the servants of the house and a few old passers-by
would listen jostling in the peristyle
and the maids at the doors, their aprons raised to their eyes,
and our mother, the mistress, in the middle of the forecourt
and next to her the nanny like an oak-tree struck by lightning
and the tutor beside them, yellow like wax in the midst of his
    thin beard,
like a dry hand clutching the strings of a harp,
and the younger daughters, still, at the windows,
hidden behind their dreams, their suspicions,
listening without comprehending,
observing the beautiful curve of the messenger's knee,
his young chestnut beard and his black hair
thick and matted from sweat and dust,
a twig of thistle caught on his tunic – So
forests walk and tables kick up in the air like horses
and triremes fly over the trees at sunset
and the oarsmen bend and rise, bend and rise, bend and rise,
surely in the rhythm of love-making; and the oars
are naked women hung by their hair
thrashing about gleaming in the sea
until the foam of the Milky Way is outlined behind the triremes.
    So then –

And the messenger was announcing the dazzling victory
out of innumerable deaths – without counting the wounded –
he was announcing finally the arrival of the master
with many spoils and banners and carriages and slaves
and a wound in the middle of his forehead – he said –
like a new marvellous eye through which death looked out,
and now the master could see into the bowels

of landscapes, of objects, of men,
as if everything were made of transparent glass and he could read
    freely
the rhythms of our blood, our moods, our fate,
the veins of gold that run in the stone,
the branches of coal spread out in the subterranean dark,
the silver nerves of water branching out in rocks,
the slight shivers of guilt under one's clothes and skin.

Everyone listened (and we too) as if turned to stone,
anxious, bent and tearless,
as if already become glass,
and they could all see, and they themselves could see themselves,
their bare skeletons in the glass, those also glass,
fragile, without any shelter. And yet

in this total exposure
in this deadly weakness
in this shadowless transparency

they felt suddenly soothed, dissolved
within the vastness of the transparency, they also vast,
as if sinless in the general sinfulness,
all like brothers in the general desert of mutual enmity
as if armed by the unarmed state of man,
beautifully, nobly dressed in universal nakedness.

'Let the master come' – said our mistress mother.
'He's welcome. He too is glass.
Glass. Glass. There it is – we also know this eye –
we have it, here, we also, in the middle of our forehead.
We too have known death well. We know. We see.
He taught us first. We were the first ones to see again.

'Welcome to the glass master with his glass sword
coming to his glass wife, his glass children,

his glass citizens, dragging behind him
flocks of glass dead, glass spoils, glass slave girls,
glass triumphs. Let the bells ring;
let fires signal from one look-out post to the other
our glass victory – yes, our own victory,
the victory of us all. Because we also fought
by means of our patience and even more so
by means of our unbearable thousand-eyed expectation. And
    those who died
they too are victors – they are the best ones – and they see.

'So, let the bells ring to the end of the horizon.
And you, slave women, why are you standing about! Prepare
the glass food, the glass wines, the glass fruit;
our glass master is coming. He's coming.'

That's how the mistress spoke and the blood
hammered on her temples, and you could see
her perspiration before it formed, before it trickled down on her
    pale blue cheeks.

The old governess who held her for a moment
when she almost fainted, stood by her now with her experienced
    silence,
covered her with her wise shadow under the big domes
of her dilated eyes. Then she shook
her black apron as if brushing away
a black bird. And the messenger left.

An owl flew low in the yard
though it was still early in the afternoon –
it was still light and the owl's shadow was imprinted indelibly
right over the gate (it's still there). The slave women ran inside
    the house.
The mistress forgot to dress her children. She went into the bath.
She filled it with hot water and she did not wash. Soon after

she locked herself in her bedroom and looking in the mirror
    made herself up
red, red, all purple, like a mask, like a dead woman, like a statue,
like a murderess or even as if already slaughtered. And the sun in
    the distance was setting

yellow and glowing like a crowned adulterer,
a gold-adorned embezzler of another's power,
furious at his cowardice and frightful in his fear
while the bells tolled madly throughout the country.

So, the slave women knew these stairs well,
years and years in this house,
and yet they uncovered their faces and looked,
and they retraced their steps for a moment, worried they'd be
    seen
and then they again covered their faces with their hands and left,
black, small, disgusting, bent,
like black dots, like malaria flies,
running under the stone rain of the peristyle,
and the big broom, left overturned behind the kitchen door
like a nightmare, hair on end, unable to scream. They all left us.

We hired charwomen to mop the stairs,
to wash the marble well, to scrub them. The marble
would sweat blood again soon after. They too went. They left us.
So we had to abandon everything – sweeping, mopping, cleaning
    away the cobwebs.
And the stone always at it – puking more and more blood.

A red river circled our house;
we were cut off from the world;
later everyone forgot about us;
they were no longer afraid of us; and we also were not afraid.
Of course, the passers-by passed at some distance,
but they wouldn't cross themselves

or spit to exorcize the ghosts.
The road nearest our house
became covered with weeds, nettles, thorns
and even with some pale blue wild flowers – it no longer looked
    like a road.

At night, if a woman delayed,
still washing at the river and you could hear the thumping of the
    beater
on the soft, soaked woven clothes, no one'd say
a knife was piercing flesh
or that a secret trap-door was being shut
or that a corpse was dumped out of the northern window into
    the moat – they'd only say
that a beater was beating the clothes,
they could even tell from the sound
whether the fabric was woollen or cotton, silk or linen
and they'd know that a woman was bleaching her daughter's
    dowry,
they'd even imagine the wedding day,
the pale groom, the blushing bride,
the two clasping bodies almost ethereal behind the tulle curtains
    of the bed
swaying in the night breeze. Such details
and also such accuracy (isn't this a sign of balance?)
along with this feeling of the indispensable,
as if what'd happened and what followed were necessary –
the feeling of the inevitable and the unaccountable, and also
a vein of music pulsing in the air
and you hear it again and you hear it again and you can't tell

where it is – a little above the trees?
under the empty benches in the garden?
in that bath? over the red river?
or in father's locked armoury full of trophies from so many vain
    wars,

or in the unused sandals of the older brother who's away, on
    boats, for years, a sailor,
and who knows if he'll ever return,
or in the sketch-books of the younger brother who's stopped
    writing from the sanatorium,
or in poor mother's wardrobe
with its long, white, pleated dresses and the broad hammered
    buckles –

(often, at night, I saw the dresses, from the window,
strolling on their own under the trees
billowing lightly like shadows in the moonlight, and behind
their white mist, behind their pale waving,
one could make out the dry fountain and its bronze dolphin
curved in an ultimate flash of escape – that transparency, glass,
that did not leave stains of guilt and memory
because memory too is useless in a continuous absence or
    presence). Anyhow,

that vein of music could be heard everywhere; and you don't
    even know
why you are happy, what happiness is; you only see
things you had never before noticed or seen,
yet free now of their weight. We knew neither the messenger,
nor the murder, nor the frightened slave women that ran,
and I was one of the two girls who stood at the two windows
and who also looked at the two girls as if from below the stairs
    or from the street,
almost from the position of the messenger, or through the eyes
    of the youngest slave girl,
it was I who stood always at the window; (I often envied the
    slave women
for their impertinence, their cunning, their gaiety and their
    freedom,
that deep freedom of slavery that saves you
from decisions and initiatives – I envied them).

Ah, I saw nothing, I remember nothing; only that fine feeling,
so finely felt, granted us by death, to see death
to its transparent depths. And the music continued
as sometimes at dawn when we wake up early for no reason,
and the air outside is so thick with the chirpings
of thousands of invisible birds – so thick and steamy
there's no room for anything else – bitterness, hope, guilt,
    memory –
and time is indifferent, a stranger,
like a stranger that passed by quietly in the street opposite
without at all taking in our house, or looking at it,
holding some opaque, unwashed panes under his armpit,
you don't know what he wants to do with them, where he's
    taking them,
what they are meant for and for what windows they're destined
and indeed you don't even wonder and you don't see him dis-
    appear either,
discreet and silent, round the last bend of the street.

Who was it then that saved all these things for us, with such
    precision, so many dimensions,
washed, pleasant, cleaned and tidied up,
flayed of all wounds and every death?
And the red river around the house – nothing –
clear water only from the other day's rain, tepid rain
reflecting the red sunset till night, until the time
when that endless glass transparency spreads around,
and you can see to its core the endless, the imperishable, the
    invisible,
you also endless, imperishable, invisible, surrounded
by the tiny whispers of furniture and stars. And our mother
    sits
on the carved chair embroidering her endless needlework
under the three-flame oil lamp, its flames quivering
from the draught between the two windows
and father has been away hunting since morning

the melancholy coil of the hunters' horn resounding in his ears
and the eager and friendly barking of the dogs.

Our youngest sister, escaping the attention of the wet-nurse,
is dreaming in the garden's cool, riding the stone lion,
and everything is so quiet –
no one was wrong, nothing happened,
only the creaking of a door below
and of the iron garden gate – maybe the milkman brought
a bowl of yoghurt for mother's diet – she's afraid of putting on
    weight,
and it is bliss for the children when mother starts watching her
    weight again,
when she looks after herself a little, when she looks at herself in
    the mirror now and then,
when she fixes her rich beautiful hair coiled in a bun; – the
    yoghurt
takes on a cool brilliance, as if marble, pale blue
under the starlight and the shadow of the trees; you can hear
the soft voice of the youngest housemaid
paying for the week's milk and she lingers on
counting the change again and again. And the garden,
at its furthest point, its darkest corner, sparkles
now and then, it shines as the big sunflowers
move their warm shoulders in the night
and a pale blue mist shimmers under the nostrils of the statues
as if the statues breathed secretly the damp fragrance from the
    roses.

Our youngest brother is always painting,
in the studio with the looms, exquisite watercolours
in the decorative manner of Minoan art – he never shows us his
    paintings –
or he draws, in the pottery studio, on small and large pitchers,
with black or brick-red lines of feigned austerity,
young warriors, or dancers hidden entirely

203

behind huge shields – if you don't look closely
you might think it's only circles, a black chain. Our older
 brother
has resigned from the royal navy; now,
always looking serious, he spends his time reading in the room
 next door. In the stillness of time
you can hear the page turn as though a secret door were opening
to a white, transparent landscape. And, yes,

just then, a door is opening. Father is coming.
The table is being laid. They are calling us.
We all go down the inside staircase.
We sit at the table and eat, listening
to the short sharp barkings of the dogs in the courtyard and to
 the voice of the foreman.

Life after all is so simple. So beautiful.
Mother leans over her plate and cries.
Father rests his arm on her shoulder.
'It is from happiness,' she excuses herself.

And we look through the open windows
at the boundless transparent night with its lean moon
like a finger forgotten among
the pale blue pages of a quiet, shut book.

It is a little cool tonight. Autumn, you see.
Tomorrow or the next day we'll shut the windows again.
Anyway, we don't have to worry about firewood – plenty of
 that –
we can get it not only from the woods but can also use our old
 furniture,
heavy doors, beams, sofas, coffins, smoking pipes, guns,
even our long-dead grandfather's carriage.

If you are going away, please tell our uncle not to worry about us.
    We are fine.
And death is soft like a mattress stuffed with wool, a feather or
    straw
mattress to which we're used; – the mattress
has taken the shape of our bodies, obliging, – a death entirely
    our own –
at least we're not deceived by death, or slighted – death is certain,
we too are certain about death – the austere, supreme certainty.

But if you're not leaving Argos, it would be a great pleasure for
    us
to see you here again. For your sake, I'll even unnail a door
to show you father's armoury,
to show you that shield on whose black metal
you can still see imprinted the reflections of a thousand poses of
    dead warriors,
to show you the finger-prints of blood, and the fountain of
    blood
and the tunnel through which, dressed as women, escaped
the twelve bearded war leaders and their pale chief
who, although dead, led them unerringly straight to the exit.
The opening, at the other end, was left uncovered,
silent, deep and dark like an unknown error.

And the evening star – did you notice it perhaps? – soft, the
    evening star,
like an eraser – it keeps rubbing at the same point
as if to erase our error – what error? –
and there's an imperceptible sound as the eraser moves back and
    forth
over the error – and the error is not erased;
small bits of paper shreds fall on the trees and sparkle;
it is a pleasant occupation – and it doesn't matter
that the error cannot be erased; the movement of the star
    suffices,

gentle, persistent and perpetual,
as if the original and final meaning – rhythm; heavenly energy,
the practical side too, like that of the loom or of verse –
back and forth, back and forth, the star among the cypress trees,
a gold dart among the long funereal threads,
now hiding, now revealing our error – not ours,
the world's error, a basic error – why should we be blamed
    for it? –
the error of birth or death – did you notice?
Autumn evenings are beautiful – reconciling –
erasing with a tame, a total guilt, the guilt of all of us,
creating a secret friendship between us,
a friendship of rhythm – yes, yes, precisely, a friendship of
    rhythm, of rhythm – that's it – back and forth, back and forth,
birth-death, love-dream, action-silence – it is a way out, I tell
    you,
to that far end, that very dark point, and then beyond that,
    straight to heaven, –

a breeze comes from there, perspiration dries – a breath, my god,
    a balm finally,
and you can hear so clearly in the night people talking on the
    roof-tops around
and the cool sound of the bucket from the garden-well
and the voice under the trees that says: 'I'll return'
and the child's panting as he unbuckles his shoes by himself for
    the first time
and the flute through the student's open window – an amateur's
    music –
a music anyway that rises and becomes one
with the superb, the vain, the coordinated music of the stars.

And, yes, I assure you, although dead, he did lead them straight
    to the exit –
no matter that we know that the way out is usually nothing but
a different, a necessary, a cunning and inevitable death.

So, please tell uncle not to worry about us
there in his wonderfully disciplined Sparta.
We too are fine here in Argos.
Only – he must realize this – this is the limit. He must realize this.

('Yes, yes,' I nodded mechanically and stood up. I could under-
stand nothing. A feeling of magic fear had seized me as if I had
been suddenly confronted by the decadence and the fascination
of a very ancient civilization. It was dark now. She took me to
the stairs lighting my way down with an old paraffin lamp.
What did she mean? And what about the dead man who led
them to the exit? Maybe ... Not, of course, Christ. And the
house – not Agamemnon's. And the younger brother with the
artistic inclinations – who was he? There was no second brother.
Then? What was this house for? And what was I trying to make
of the words of a mad woman? I was outside. I walked fast and
hearing my steps I stopped. Something astringent and unsatisfied
remained on my tongue, diluted in my saliva by all this black
vagueness, as if I had bitten into a cypress cone. And yet I also felt
something solid, rich, clean which made me euphoric, which
helped me think with mathematical precision how easily I would
overcome difficulties in my work tomorrow, difficulties that had
always seemed insuperable till now. A huge moon had risen
among the cypress trees. Behind me I could sense the dark mass
of that house like an imposing ancient tomb. And, if nothing else,
I had at least learned what I had to avoid, what we have to avoid.)

Athens
September 1959